Academic Version

Erika Matulich

W9-BCR-992

MarketingBuilder

From the JIAN family of best-selling and award-winning software

Express

JIAN Tools For Sales, Inc.
1975 W. El Camino Real, Suite 301
Mountain View, CA 94040-2218
415.254.5600
415.254.5642 Fax

SOUTH-WESTERN College Publishing

An International Thomson Publishing Company

Publishing Team Director: John Szilagyi
Project Leader: Susan Freeman Carson
Text Development and Production: The Oxford Associates, Inc.
Production Editor: Kelly Keeler
Cover Design: Tin Box Studio/Sandy Weinstein
Cover Photo: © J. Craig Sweat Photography
Marketing Manager: Steve Scoble

JIAN Tools for Sales, Inc.

Founded by Burke Franklin in his living room in 1986, JIAN began operations as a provider of sales and marketing brochures and direct mail vehicles. Two years later, it introduced the revolutionary BizPlan*Builder* software, winner of Success Magazine's "Editor's Choice Gold Medal Award." BizPlan*Builder*, the flagship of JIAN's line, provides business and marketing plan templates for organizing and financing a business. Now the most popular business plan software ever, BizPlan*Builder* has sold nearly twice as many copies as any competitive product, over 300,000 copies.

What is a Jian? You might think of it this way: while a Black Belt is a master of the martial arts, a "Jian" is a master of every art—the ultimate human with extraordinary acumen, power and resourcefulness. JIAN's mission is to provide strategic building blocks to help managers build better companies—faster, easier and more economically.

All JIAN packages are developed and refined by experts with successful, real-world business experience. JIAN has gathered input from these specialists as well as commissioned accountants, consultants, lawyers and other experts for further guidance. Most of the people at JIAN, as well as the consultants and independent contractors who work for JIAN, are or have been owners of small companies. All of these materials, insights and experience have been engineered into tools and templates you can use to build your business.

JIAN continues to meet the needs of new and emerging businesses with innovative new software products including:

- BizPlan*Builder*
- EmployeeManual*Maker*
- Publicity*Builder*
- Loan*Builder*
- Agreement*Builder*
- LivingTrust*Builder*
- SafetyPlan*Builder*

Welcome to MarketingBuilder Express

Why have a compass in the wild? Why have a rudder on a ship? Why do you need skills in market planning and strategy? Because marketing is one of the most important driving forces in any company. It supports the sales of products. A marketing plan provides a stable base from which a company can enter the rough and competitive marketplace. Since effective marketing is a key to running a successful business, consistency, clarity, and goal orientation in marketing activities are very important. A written plan will help everyone in marketing, and in the company in general, understand and work toward common goals.

We designed this marketing planning process and software to guide you as you learn to plan and implement marketing strategy. With the help of MarketingBuilder *Express*, you will complete a marketing plan that will enable you to effectively identify the resources needed to promote and position products in the competitive marketplace.

MarketingBuilder *Express* is a steamlined version of the original, full-length version of JIAN's MarketingBuilder. This shorter version allows you to complete the essential elements of a marketing plan in less time.

Let's Get Started

MarketingBuilder *Express* is designed to be effective for a broad spectrum of businesses across a variety of industries. Your instructor will direct you in the selection of a company you can use to develop a marketing plan project.

MarketingBuilder *Express* software templates enable you to generate a unique plan and to be confident that you have a well-thought-out strategy for managing resources and people to meet the challenges of the future. Templates are also provided in worksheet form so you can work in the environment of your choice to complete your plan.

MarketingBuilder *Express* has background information, instructions, software templates and worksheets for preparing each section of your marketing plan:

- Market Analysis
- Marketing Communications
- Sales Plan

The templates lead you through the thought process and writing process for each section. The templates have complete sentences with blanks for you to fill in for your business. When you finish a template for a section, you have all the text needed for that section. Of course, as you progress you will naturally edit, update and refine the text. If a particular passage or section doesn't make sense to you or doesn't seem appropriate for your business, then simply cross it out.

The **Introduction** explains the differences between marketing and sales and explains how a marketing plan is used and why it's important to have a plan. Included in this section are the Top 20 Questions you're most likely to be asked about your business. Be sure to read the introduction before starting on your marketing plan. Page 1.

Part 1, **Market Analysis**. The chapters in Part 1 have reference information and advice covering every aspect of market analysis. After you research your market, you should have a clear idea of who your customers are and what they want, who your competitors are and what they are doing, what your product offers consumers, how different prices affect your ability to sell, and the risks you face in marketing your products. Page 5.

Part 2, **Marketing Communications**, is about using the information you collect in Part 1 to develop a successful marketing communications plan. It has advice about the key methods for reaching your market, including sales promotions, sales literature, advertising, public relations, trade shows and customer service. Page 59.

Part 3, **Sales Plan,** has information, instructions, and a template for writing your company's internal sales plan. Page 113.

Appendix A, **Using MarketingBuilder *Express***, has instructions for installing and using the MarketingBuilder *Express* templates. Page 148.

Appendix B, **Resources**, lists resources you can use to develop your marketing plan. Page 152.

Appendix C, **References**, is a list of books and articles about marketing. Page 157.

There's also an index. Page 159.

Internet Access

Take a look at our web site! You'll find a variety of useful information, including new products, demos, listings of professional advisors, and links to complementary products and services. You'll find us at `http://www.jianusa.com`.

Using MarketingBuilder Express in the Classroom

The best way for you to progress through MarketingBuilder *Express* is to select a real-world company, product, or service and complete a marketing plan for that firm. To make issues even more important, contact that firm and present the marketing plan to them at the end of the semester. This client relationship encourages the best level of critical thinking, problem solving, and concept application. Small businesses are an excellent source of clients. Appendix B has a list of product businesses, service businesses, and not-for-profit organizations. Or you may decide to make up your own product or service that realistically could be launched at the end of the semester. The Objectives, Questions, and Activities included with each chapter are designed to help you build your knowledge as you build your plan.

You can also use MarketingBuilder *Express*, as well as the original Marketing*Builder*, to complete the Marketing Plan activities in Lamb, Hair, McDaniel's *Marketing*, 4E.

MarketingBuilder Express Software

The MarketingBuilder *Express* software package included with this book consists of word processing and spreadsheet templates that work easily with most popular Microsoft Windows programs. You can print the completed templates and use them as your actual marketing plan.

Throughout this text, you'll find icons like the one shown here. These icons indicate MarketingBuilder *Express* templates.

MarketingBuilder Express Contents

x

*Always bear in mind that your own resolution
to succeed is more important than any other thing.*

—*Abraham Lincoln*

Introduction

Marketing includes all the actions your business takes to understand who potential customers are and what they want, to let them know about your product, and to make obtaining the product easy. Effective marketing can greatly influence your overall success. A comprehensive, well thought-out marketing plan can be one of the most important documents you create.

This reference guide will help you understand many different aspects of marketing. Some may apply to your current business, others may not. MarketingBuilder *Express* will be your guide to making informed decisions about your company's marketing direction, and then to taking appropriate, effective action.

In the following pages, we look at the importance of marketing in a company and outline the general parts of a marketing plan. This introduction gives you an overview of the marketing plan and the interrelationship of the three sections of your marketing plan.

Please note that in MarketingBuilder *Express*, whenever we refer to your "product," we are referring to either your product or service. If you are a service business, your service is, after all, the product you provide.

■ What Marketing Is

Marketing is all the activities that are involved in moving goods from the producer to the consumer, including market research, pricing, sales, packaging, shipping, advertising, and more. The purpose of marketing is to find out who wants or needs your product and under what conditions they will buy it. It is directly or indirectly involved in every aspect of a business because the purpose of a business is almost always to sell. If a company's marketing is not functioning correctly, other aspects of the business will likely not function properly.

■ Why Write a Marketing Plan?

Why do you need a marketing plan? Because marketing is one of your company's most important driving forces. It supports the sales of your products. A marketing plan provides a stable base from which your company can enter the rough and competitive marketplace. Because effective marketing is a key to running a successful business, consistency, clarity, and goal orientation in your marketing activities are very important. A written plan will help everyone in marketing, and in your company in general, understand and work toward common goals.

Marketing is one of the most expensive and complicated components of your business. Once set in motion, most of your activities will be difficult, if not impossible, to change or reverse if you've made a mistake or need to change strategies down the road.

The process of writing a marketing plan allows you to examine the inner workings of your company's revenue generator, sales. A comprehensive marketing plan serves as a benchmark for your company by establishing concrete and current objectives, strategies, and tactics. Once a marketing plan is written, it will serve as a record that will help your company learn from experience. And, most importantly, your marketing plan allows your company to enter the marketplace with its eyes wide open to possibilities and problems.

■ Your Marketing Plan Format

Marketing plans, as business plans, can be presented in many different ways. The plan can be a formal written document or a casual verbal presentation. Most businesses need a written marketing plan because of the scope of tasks involved. It would simply be impossible to verbally convey all the information to every person who needs to carry out the activities.

As with all written documents, a clear, consistent style works best. The worksheets in MarketingBuilder *Express* provide subject headings, outlines, and expert advice for easy reference. No matter who receives copies of your plan, it should be neatly and professionally presented.

■ Getting Started

Your marketing plan has three main sections:

1. Market Analysis—understanding who potential customers are and what they want

2. Marketing Communications—letting them know about your product

3. Sales Plan—making it easy for them to obtain your product

Each section can stand alone if you want a narrower marketing plan (or if you want to divide responsibility for developing the plan), but they are designed to function together.

MarketingBuilder *Express* will help you create an internal document that addresses the many marketing and sales functions your company must consider. In certain situations, you may wish to customize your internal document to a version suitable for presentation to people outside your company. Parts 1, 2, and 3 focus on the three main sections of your marketing plan and include comprehensive worksheets to help you effectively design your marketing plan.

Each part is divided into chapters with background information and a discussion of your options. The purpose of these discussions is not to tell you what to do or what is best, but to help you think through the different possibilities. You know your company best.

And finally, don't look at this as a grueling, painful process. We've presented the questions; all you need to do is to come up with the answers. Enjoy getting to know your company better and making it more successful.

It is a good idea to understand where your company is now before you try to decide where you are going. The following *Top 20 Questions* worksheet allows you to "put your finger on the pulse" of your business. Use this questionnaire as a mirror to reflect the face of your company, and to help you focus on what is needed before you create your marketing plan.

■ Top 20 Questions – Worksheet

The Top 20 Questions are what most people will ask you about your business. MarketingBuilder *Express* helps you develop and enhance your responses to these questions.

The answers to these questions can be used to create an initial summary of the status of your business, which can be used as source material for your marketing and sales materials (e.g., brochures, advertisements, company backgrounder, etc.).

QUESTION.DOC

Note: Word processing templates are shown with the .DOC extension. Depending on which installation option you select, your files may have the extension .RTF . See details in Appendix A.

1. What type of business do you have?

2. What is the purpose of your business?

3. Who are your target customers?

4. What is your primary product? (If you offer more than one product, focus on your primary ones.)

5. What is the primary function of your product?

6. What are three unique benefits of your product?

7. What is your reason for being in this business? (What's a nice person like you doing in a business like this?)

8. What led you to develop your product?

9. Who is your competition? (List both direct and indirect competitors.)

10. How is your product different from that of your competition?

11. What are the top three objections to buying your product immediately? (Address any possible objections up front. This will keep you from having to be on the defensive, acting as if you overlooked something or have something to hide.)

12. What is the pricing of your product versus your competition?

13. When did you first offer your product or when will your product be available?

14. Is this product used in connection with other products?

15. Are you making any special offers to distributors or customers?

16. What is the key message or phrase that describes your business? (Try to keep the key message to one sentence.)

17. What are your current plans for advertising and promoting your product?

18. Do you have datasheets, brochures, diagrams, sketches, photographs, related press releases, or other documentation about your product? (List all of your marketing collateral materials. If you do not currently have any, determine what materials you will develop and the dates when you will have them available.)

19. How will your marketing assist the growth of your business?

20. Do you have the marketing and sales management expertise needed to achieve your business goals? (List the names of your sales and marketing managers and their qualifications.)

A wise man makes more opportunities than he finds.

—*Francis Bacon*

Part 1: Market Analysis

Part 1 of MarketingBuilder *Express* introduces the basic activities of market analysis, helps you define and understand the existing marketplace where your company competes or plans to compete, and provides tips to find the necessary market information.

The result will be a market analysis that is the cornerstone for all your marketing efforts, and the basis for the marketing communications and sales parts of your plan. Market analysis provides the knowledge on which the rest of your marketing plan will be based.

Chapter 1

How Do You Analyze a Market?

No matter what type of business you are in, the final decision to buy or not to buy your product is made by an individual or group of individuals—this is your market. The better you understand your market, and the forces at work within it, the more successful your business will be.

Large companies can usually allocate more resources to market analysis than smaller companies. In either case, even a cursory market analysis will improve your ability to make good marketing decisions and to be more competitive in the marketplace.

Most companies engage in some kind of market analysis, even though they may not call it that. Noticing whether a certain product's sales have risen since you lowered the price or seeing that your new store has higher sales than the others is a form of market analysis. MarketingBuilder *Express* helps you formalize those findings by writing them down and placing them in the larger context of your business. The point is to do more than notice trends. You also need to understand why they happen and how you can influence in a positive way the course your business takes.

 **Learning Objectives**

After completing this chapter, you should be able to:

1. Understand what a market is

2. Know the components of a Market Analysis

3. Be familiar with trends in the 1990s

■ Identify Your Target Market

Knowing your target market—who you are selling to—is critical for positioning your company and product in the marketplace. Instead of saying, "I sell greeting cards," you should be able to say, "I sell greeting cards for birthdays and major holidays that appeal to 25- to 40-year-old single, professional men." The better you understand the dynamics and quirks of your target market, the more successful you will be in selling to it.

You must also have a good idea where you fit in the market. A market profile will help you determine a niche for your product, room for growth, and the size of the market that you are working in. A profile of your target market will help you choose your marketing communications and sales activities. The more you know about your target market, the more effectively you will compete. On the other hand, defining your target market does not mean that you do not, or should not, sell your product in other markets. You probably do have customers in more than one market.

Your target market, however, is where the bulk of your profits are derived. You reach customers in your target market more efficiently and cost effectively than customers in your secondary markets. You know them better and often they know you better. Customers in your target market are generally the most profitable customers, and you can always use more of them.

Twenty percent of all customers generate eighty percent of demand. It makes solid business sense to focus a large part of your marketing resources and efforts to target your most profitable and influential customers.

■ Profile Your Customers

Creating a customer profile can save your company a lot of time and money. Knowing your customer will shape the kinds of market schemes you want to undertake and the types of sales strategies that are likely to be most successful. An advertising campaign that appeals to your specific target audience will bring in more sales than a great campaign that is loved by a broad range of people who would never buy your product.

■ Know Your Competitors

Today, most markets are extremely competitive, and only the best-informed companies with the best products will survive. Because your competitors are going after the same market you are, you should always know what they are up to. You want to position your product on the market with your competitors in mind. The more you know about your competitors, the better. Have they advertised? How have they packaged their product? What is their sales literature like? If you can find your competitors' weakness, you can fill the gap they have left.

Remember, just as you are looking at other companies' successes and failures, they are watching yours. If you leave any gaps, you can be sure another company will try to fill those gaps.

■ Understand Your Product

To position your product on the market, you must understand it as an outsider would, not just as an enamored parent. There are different ways to find out how your product is perceived in the market, such as through surveys or tests, but you can begin simply by taking a critical look at your product. Be as objective as possible.

Knowing your product will help you portray it honestly and positively. You should never lie about the quality or performance of your product, but you can choose to highlight its strongest features in your promotions.

If you find weaknesses, ask yourself how they impact your product. There may be a simple way to adjust your product to make it better. Or you can decide to go ahead and sell a product that you know is great in most ways but has one little problem, and be ready with answers to complaints.

■ Set the Right Price

Price is an extremely important factor in positioning your product on the market. Price is often the first thing a potential customer looks at. Many factors, from your break-even level to your competitors' prices, need to be taken into account when pricing. Understanding the consequences of several different pricing structures to your customers will assist you in finding the best price for overall success.

One thing you should always keep in mind is that consumers do not like prices to rise, so try to come up with a price that is realistic and that you will not have to raise in the short term. If a price does not allow you to break even, you have to consider what the consequences will be when you raise your prices. Thinking different options through before product release will help you find the best one.

■ Analyze Your Risks

Risk is part of any business. Thoroughly analyzing the risks of your business will help you plan for and avoid problems. The purpose of identifying risks is to have a fuller picture of what you are undertaking. There are two types of risk that most businesses face: business risk and environmental risk.

Business Risk

Many risks involved in starting and running a business have to do with your actual business operations. There is always a risk that you won't be able to sell your product or that sales will fall far short of your goals. This is a clear risk for most businesses and one reason companies carry out market analysis. If you have thoroughly analyzed your market and know the characteristics of your customers, you have less risk of failure. With accurate information in these areas, you can usually take very tangible steps to minimize your business risks.

Environmental Risk

Environmental risks are things you have little control over, such as the state of the economy, the weather, and government regulation. For example, you can't control the weather, but you can determine the effects of bad weather on your business and possible adjustments you can make. If you make canned tomato soup, you need a steady supply of tomatoes. Bad weather could ruin tomato crops and limit your supply or raise prices. To determine your risk, ask yourself who your suppliers are, where they grow tomatoes, and how steady their crops have been for the past five or ten years.

■ Review Questions

1. What is a market?

2. Why is it important to perform a market analysis?

3. What are the areas examined in a market analysis?

■ Activities

1. Identify the key competitors for your business. List their strengths and weaknesses. How will you position your service or product to take advantage of your competitors' weaknesses?

2. Research trends into the next century that are most critical to success or failure of your business.

Chapter 2

Your Target Market

This chapter describes the components necessary to carry out a thorough analysis of your target market. To analyze a target market, you should be familiar with the industry, market segments, niche markets, and a S.W.O.T. analysis.

Learning Objectives

After completing this chapter, you should be able to:

1. Understand the specifics of your industry

2. Define the market segment you want to sell to

3. Recognize specialty market niches within your market

4. Perform a S.W.O.T. analysis

5. Thoroughly describe your target market

■ Industry Analysis

An industry analysis begins with collecting information about the size, growth rate, and structure of your industry, such as information technology, tourism, food, or transportation. Next, you should examine the companies and products that are successful in your industry. What makes them successful? How do they stand out? How are other industry players marketing their products? What tactics are they using? Also look at companies and products that are not successful. What do you think is holding back their sales? The industry probably existed before you entered the market and there may be valuable lessons to learn from the past. The information you gather about your industry past and present will help you monitor changes and trends in the marketplace and may show you an opening place for your product.

You can find information about your industry in trade journals, from your chamber of commerce, through online services, and in the public library's business section.

■ Market Segment

It is essential to define the segment of the market you want to sell to. There is not one specific way to define a market segment. Defining a market segment is simply narrowing a broader market by certain criteria, such as geographic location, income, age group, and desires. The narrower the segment you define, the more directly you can target that group.

You should not, however, eliminate potential customers by defining too narrow a target market. You may decide to target two or more segments of a market. If you are targeting several different segments, you will need to take several different approaches to promotion, pricing, and distribution.

The auto industry is part of the transportation industry. Within the auto industry are distinct market segments. If you sell Mercedes Benzes, you are in the luxury car segment and will target higher income customers. A Kia dealer who sells inexpensive, small, practical cars will sell to a very different clientele. Kia could further define its market segment as, for example, young professional women between 25 and 35, who earn between $30,000 and $60,000. Once you have this definition, you can gear your marketing efforts to reach that group.

Look at a market segment's size and growth characteristics. How large is the market segment you have defined? How many competitors are there? How much do you expect that segment to grow? At what rate do you expect that segment to grow?

In defining your market segment, look at who your customers are, the kind of products they are buying, and when they are buying those products (if they are seasonal). Sources such as industry analyses, census reports, and trade journal studies will help you define and understand your market segment.

■ Niche Markets

Some market segments are so small, they are considered "niche markets." Often, smaller companies find niches they can fill that larger companies would not bother to enter because the return is too small. For example, if your product is bread, your segment may be health breads with whole grains. You could then define your niche by aiming at customers who want only organic ingredients in healthful breads. A large company that makes bread may consider the organic bread market too small to enter. If you do define a market niche, consider what demand that niche holds and whether there will be enough return from that niche to make it worthwhile.

■ S.W.O.T. Analysis

A broad-based S.W.O.T. Analysis can be a quick and easy way to examine your company. It involves looking at your company's **S**trengths, **W**eaknesses, **O**pportunities, and **T**hreats.

If you understand the S.W.O.T. elements of your company and your industry, your strategies for placing yourself and your product in the market will be much more successful. Identifying your company's primary strengths, weaknesses, opportunities, and threats will allow you to put into place appropriate marketing strategies.

Strengths and Weaknesses

Most companies and products have strengths and weaknesses, and many businesses forget to look at them, which itself is a weakness. If you examine your own company and product for strengths and weaknesses, you can successfully place your product on the market. By also looking at your competitors' strengths and weaknesses, you can position your product so that your strengths shine through and convey that your product is strong where the competition's product is weak. Finally, your company may have different strengths depending on your target market, and identifying your weaknesses helps you define a realistic target market.

Opportunities

An important part of success in business is finding unexploited opportunities. In fact, most new businesses probably have found an unexploited opportunity or they wouldn't go into business in the first place. Companies must remain dynamic to survive, and a market analysis may help you continue to find new and unexploited opportunities.

These new opportunities may be in the form of demand for a new, yet similar product. Or, maybe you will find a whole group of potential customers that is not served through other companies' channels.

Threats

Analyzing potential threats that could come from your choosing a particular target market will help you decide if you have found the right market. If your target market is very price sensitive, this could be a threat if another company can beat your price. Another type of threat is if your product is easy to copy. Some companies might wait for you to come up with new products and then simply copy them. Because those companies would not have spent much money on research and development, they might be able to undercut your price and take customers away from you. Another threat could come in the form of a deep-pocketed potential competitor looming on your target market horizon. If you know what threats there are in choosing a certain target market, you can better evaluate whether you should enter it.

Once you have matched your market and segment(s) with your own strengths and weaknesses through a S.W.O.T. Analysis, you can begin to define who your customers will be. As you paint this picture, you can better design your marketing efforts to reach those people. You can also set goals and objectives that are based on the defined market.

■ Target Market Checklist

✓ Have you examined the history, size, structure, and growth rate of your industry?

✓ Have you examined why the successful companies and products in your industry are successful? Have you looked at the unsuccessful companies and products?

✓ Have you defined your market segment or segments? Have you studied your market segments (growth characteristics, competitors, etc.)?

✓ Have you examined your strengths and weaknesses and those of your competitors?

✓ Have you searched for new and unexploited opportunities for marketing your product or service?

✓ Have you considered the potential threats of your intended target market?

■ Review Questions

1. What is a target market?

2. Can you sell to customers who are not in your defined target market?

3. What information should you collect for an industry analysis?

4. What criteria can be used to help define a market segment?

5. How should a market segment be described?

6. What is the difference between a market segment and a market niche?

7. What are the components of a S.W.O.T. analysis?

■ Activities

1. For your business, identify the industry it operates in and describe aspects of the industry, including competing companies or products in this industry. Fill in the Industry Analysis portion of the Market Analysis template (1-MKTANL.DOC) to assist you.

2. Using several criteria (such as geographic location, age, or benefits sought), identify as many different market segments as reasonable for your business. Are any of these segments niche markets? Fill in the Market Segment portion of the Market Analysis template (1-MKTANL.DOC) to assist you.

3. Perform a brief S.W.O.T. analysis for your company. Fill in the Strengths, Weaknesses, Opportunities, and Threats sections of the Market Analysis template (1-MKTANL.DOC) to assist you.

Chapter 3

Your Customer

Your customers rule the fate of your business—whether they buy from you can make or break your company. Of course, you have a lot of control over what you offer your customer and, in that sense, you control your own destiny. Knowing who your customers are and what they want can help you gain the success you want.

By identifying your customers and their characteristics, you can gear your marketing efforts specifically toward them. Often, the difference between success and failure of your product will depend on how you market it, not on the actual product itself. A wonderful product could fail if it is sold through the wrong channel or advertised to the wrong group. Marketing the same product to a specific set of customers will increase the likelihood that you will succeed. You should also consider whether your customer has a particular buying cycle. If you are selling camping equipment, your customer is most likely to buy in the spring and summer. It is important to gear your marketing efforts to reaching your customers at the time they will buy.

 **Learning Objectives**

After completing this chapter, you should be able to:

1. Describe potential customers according to demographics and psychographics

2. Describe potential customers in terms of geographics and biographics

3. Understand the consumer adoption process and characteristics of consumer adopters

4. Identify economic factors that might influence the purchase habits of customers

5. Recognize the influencers of your target customer

In addition to identifying your current customer base, try to find out why some potential customers have not become customers. You can gain insight into why some people have not taken the step to buy your product by asking your current customers why they did choose your product. To obtain this information, put customer survey cards in your products or have your salespeople ask your customers questions and fill out surveys after the sale.

A customer profile describes what you know about your customers in a structured and coherent way. The customer profile for consumer markets may include the following.

■ Demographics: Who's Out There

Demographics supply information about a specific population, including age, gender, average income, ethnic background, and family makeup. Demographics are based on findings from a national census, local government agencies, and private firms whose specific task is to find out information about a population's characteristics. These studies can be conducted on a national scale and are general in scope, or they can focus on a particular metropolitan area, or be separated by ZIP Code.

Many businesses do market research by asking customers for their ZIP Code when they pay. This method not only provides you with a profile of where your customers live but also tells you what people from different areas buy. You may find that the majority of your customers come from four different ZIP Codes and that people from one ZIP Code spend 50 percent more than people from the other ones. With this information, you can better target direct mail campaigns and other promotions.

Accurate and up-to-date demographic information can be of great help to your marketing efforts. If you know that a particular area has an average annual family income of $20,000, you probably wouldn't want to sell your hand-engraved silverware there. You may, however, want to put up a billboard there for your discount supermarket. Also, if you find the average age is 35, you wouldn't want to advertise senior citizen cruises in the neighborhood newspaper.

In addition to specific demographic information about your particular target group, larger demographic trends are also important. An example of an important demographic change is the trend of women in the workplace. Because women have increased purchasing power, companies have started to target products at women that are not female-specific. In other words, marketers have long aimed perfume ads at women but only recently created car commercials aimed at the female market. This is the type of trend to be aware of so you don't miss a whole potential market.

You can obtain demographic information from your local chamber of commerce, the local newspaper, your state department of commerce, the Internet, and the local library.

■ Psychographics: Lifestyle Considerations

Demographics tell only part of the story about your customers. The rest of the story can be filled in by looking into the consumer's mind. Psychographics is the study of a particular population's values, attitudes, lifestyles, and interests. Having this information helps you determine, or at least make an intelligent guess about, the factors that motivate your potential customers to buy. Customers' lifestyles, needs, personalities, and interests usually reflect their values and attitudes. Sometimes, people who fit into one neat demographic group—say, people who earn more than $100,000 annually—can be very different in their activities, interests, and opinions.

It is also helpful to try to identify any cultural or environmental biases that may influence purchasing decisions. If you enter international markets, cultural differences, as well as language differences, will be key. When Chevrolet introduced its Nova in Latin America, it failed to take into account that the name, split in half into No-va, means "doesn't go" in Spanish. This kind of error can be avoided if a real effort is made to understand where and to whom you are selling.

■ Geographics: Where Are You?

Geographics relates to where your target market is located. Your market may be local, regional, national, or international. You must know where your customer is so you can make sure your product gets there and has a strong presence.

The larger your market, the more flexible you will have to be in your marketing efforts. You may need to keep your pricing flexible, because customers in New York City will expect to pay more than customers in Omaha. You may also have to adapt your advertising campaign or promotion strategies to fit the region, you are selling.

■ Biographics: When You Do and How You Do

Biographics describe how your customer purchases products. Do your customers pay with cash, check, or credit card? Do they order by phone or buy in person? When do they usually make purchases? Do they have a particular buying behavior or purchasing pattern? How often do they buy? Do they favor a certain product over another in the same category? How much is their average purchase?

The answers to some or all of these questions can direct your marketing efforts. If your target consumer tends to make purchases on weekends, then you would want to place your print ads in the Saturday morning paper so that your product will be fresh in the consumer's mind. Of course, you want to know if your target customer reads the paper and which one. If your customers tend to order by phone, you should consider setting up a phone order system. If your customers favor your product over the competition's, how do you keep their allegiance?

■ Consumer Adoption Process: "Wrap it up, I'll take it!"

The consumer adoption process is based on the notion that different people will accept and use your product at different stages. Consumers have adopted your product when they start to use it regularly. There are several steps consumers have to go through in the adoption process. First, they must become aware that your product exists. Then, they must be interested in the product, so that they make the effort to find out more about it and evaluate it. After they evaluate it, they will decide whether to buy it or not.

There are many factors that influence the rate at which consumers adopt products; some of them are presented below. You should think about how these factors affect your customer as you develop your marketing activities.

Relative Advantage

What advantages does your product provide the user? What does your product offer that the competition's doesn't? Will using your product make the consumer's life easier? Will it increase their chances of success? Your product needs to stand out in some way so that it inspires customers to choose it.

Compatibility

Is your product compatible with the consumer's life? In other words, will it be easy to integrate your product or will they have to buy extra items or change the way they do other things?

Complexity

How difficult is your product to understand and use? Consumers tend to like things that they can easily understand and use. If your product is complex, be aware of that and try to simplify its use.

Communicability

Can your product's uses and advantages be easily communicated? The more clearly you describe your product on its packaging and in sales literature, the more easily your customers will be able to explain that to others.

Cost

What is the initial cost of your product, and are future purchases necessary? The higher the cost of your product, the more cautious consumers will be and the more the above factors will come into play. If your product costs only 99 cents, the consumer will not give much thought to the purchase. As the price goes up, the consumer will need to be more convinced that they need your product.

Divisibility

How easily can your product be tried or sampled before the customer actually has to buy it? If you sell cereal, create small test boxes that you give away in the market or through the mail. That way the customer has nothing to lose by trying your product. If you sell cars, you obviously can't give away samples. You can, however, offer test drives.

■ Consumer Adopters

People differ greatly in their willingness to buy new products. People are also often willing to try certain new products while they stick to the old version of others. You need to consider your product and try to figure out who is most likely to buy it. If you are introducing a brand-new product, you should look at the adoption characteristics (demographics, psychographics, etc.) of innovators and early adopters, and target your initial marketing efforts at them. If you are entering a mature market, you should understand the early and late majority's characteristics.

The different groups of adopters and the percent of the total market they represent, beginning with those most willing to try new products, are:

- Innovators, 2.5%
- Early adopters, 13.5%
- Early majority, 34%
- Late majority, 34%
- Laggards, 16%

These groups usually have different traits that identify them, including social and ethnic background, age, race, family stage, and geographic location.

Innovators

Innovators tend to be young and well educated. They can understand and apply technical information in their decision-making process. They also tend to be a mobile group and have significant contacts outside their local social group. They typically rely on impersonal, scientific information rather than emotional promotions. Innovators are likely to be the first to buy your product if it is new and different.

Early Adopters

Early adopters also tend to be younger, more mobile, and more creative than people in the later stages of the adoption process. They often take leadership positions and influence others. Typically, they respond better to direct sales and are an extremely important class of consumers because of the respect they get from other consumers.

This is the group of consumers that is likely to recommend your product to others if they like it. They are also likely to be in leadership positions where they influence and decide what to buy for a company or organization. This is a good group to target because their allegiance may bring your company long-term benefits.

Early Majority

The early majority is more cautious. This group likes to avoid risk and usually waits until early adopters accept a new product. By the time the early majority is buying your product, the product is probably already into the growth stage. Typically, the early majority consists of company employees with young families. Their ability to accept risk is limited because they are usually relatively new to the workforce, and they need to spend their money on children and establish net worth.

Late Majority

The late majority are older than the early majority. They are skeptical. They have seen some of life's low points and are more cautious about trying new things. It is often only social pressure that forces them to adopt a new product. People in this category tend to ignore promotional messages and rely on other late adopters to guide them.

Laggards

For a marketer, laggards are almost a lost cause. They tend to be older, less educated, and low-income earners. They usually stick to the same product, even when the majority of consumers have changed to new products. They do not respond to marketing messages and look only to other laggards for guidance. Laggards do buy, so they shouldn't be completely discounted. However, if you are introducing a new, innovative product, look elsewhere.

■ Economic Factors

Consumers' economic standing has a direct effect on how much money they spend. Knowing your target consumers' economic circumstances can help you decide how much money to spend on them. For example, if you know someone has a lot of money to spend on leisure items, you should make a greater effort to reach that person than someone with less income. However, not all big savers are big spenders.

You may see an opportunity, though, in a market for your product among lower-income consumers. If they want to buy a product and your competitor charges a high price, maybe you can adapt the item to lower its cost and tap into a whole new market. Don't go for only the big spenders, because your product might be a hit with the many people who aren't.

Another economic factor is personal debt. Personal debt includes car loans, home mortgages, and credit card balances. The more debt consumers have, the less money they have to spend on new items today. Heavy debt limits a consumer's ability to borrow additional money for larger items, such as cars and homes. Knowing consumers' debt situations can help you understand their actions during different economic times.

Consumers spend money based on their expectations of future income, prices, inflation, and product availability. If people expect prices to rise, they will purchase things now that they feel they will need later. Similarly, if they know a product is high in demand and short in supply, they may buy that product before it becomes unavailable or exceedingly overpriced.

■ Influencers

Another factor involved in understanding your customer is knowing who influences that person. There are people who will:

- **Initiate** the inquiry for your product
- **Influence** the decision to buy
- **Decide** which product to buy
- **Permit** the purchase to be made

Try to make your product appeal to all these influential people. An example of someone who might **initiate** the inquiry for your product would be the CEO who wants to buy new office furniture. If the CEO tells the office manager to look for your brand, the first step toward purchasing your product has been taken.

Children provide a good example of people who **influence** the decision to buy. Parents usually do the actual purchasing of items for their children, but children make requests. Advertisements for toys and games are usually aimed at kids themselves even though they are not the purchasers. Because children end up using the product, they have a great deal of influence over what is bought.

The person who **decides** which product to buy could be the initiator or a different person. In the first example, the office manager may present the CEO with three different options, and the CEO will make the final decision. In a different scenario, the office manager would make the decision of which product to buy, based on the CEO's stated desires. The person who decides could also be the one who influences the parents about what to buy. Depending on the parents and the product, the parents might let a child decide which toy or game to buy.

The **permitter** is the person who has final say about whether a product will be bought. In a company, this person is probably the Chief Financial Officer (CFO), especially if it is a large purchase. The way to make sure that this person is happy is to prove that your product offers value. The way you present your product is the way it will be presented to the permitter, so be sure to stress its value.

■ Customer Checklist

✓ Have you identified your current customer base?

✓ Have you tried to find out why some potential customers have not become customers?

✓ Have you studied the demographics of your customer base?

✓ Have you studied their psychographics—their lifestyle?

✓ Have you considered geographic issues related to your customer base?

✓ Have you studied the biographics of buying, that is, how your customers purchase your products?

✓ Have you thought about your product in terms of the consumer adoption process? Have you considered which consumer group is most likely to buy your product?

✓ How much do you know about your target customers' economic circumstances?

✓ Have you thought about the people who influence your customers?

■ Review Questions

1. Why is it important to describe your customer?

2. What demographic factors can you use to describe a target market?

3. What are psychographics? How can psychographics help describe customers?

4. Why is it important that you know the geographics of your customer?

5. What are biographics? Why is it necessary to know this about customers?

6. Describe the different factors that help or hinder the consumer adoption process. Use the concept of a video-picture telephone to describe these factors.

7. What are the different categories of adopters? Which category should the marketer target and why?

8. How do economic factors influence a consumer's decision to buy?

9. Assume you wish to have a new, small refrigerator for your apartment, dorm, or office. Use specific examples of other people having different influencing roles on your purchase decision.

■ Activities

1. Profile your customer according to demographics, psychographics, geographics, biographics, and economic factors. Also indicate adopter profile and identify other possible influencers. Use the Customer Profile portion of the Market Analysis template (1-MKTANL.DOC).

2. Make a customer list of existing customers. Use the Customer Profile portion of the Market Analysis template (1-MKTANL.DOC).

Chapter 4

Your Competitors

Do you know who your competition is? In a general sense, *everyone* is your competition because *everyone* wants to lure consumers to buy their products. For example, a stereo equipment store doesn't only compete with other stereo equipment stores. It also competes with travel agents, restaurants, clothing stores, and just about anything else. Chapter 4 covers the issues and areas you should study about your competition.

It is important to know as much as possible about your competitor's business. Knowing your competitor helps you to understand your own company and its position in the marketplace. Remember, there are also future competitors around. You should try to keep tabs on who might enter your market and compete for your customers. This information will not always be easy to find, so follow developments in your industry and keep abreast of new directions companies may take that would affect your business. Following are some of the aspects of your competitor's business that you should examine and compare to your own.

 **Learning Objectives**

After completing this chapter, you should be able to:

1. Identify what your competitors offer

2. Understand the competition's price, packaging, place, and promotion

3. Recognize competitors' service policies such as delivery and customer relations

4. Classify competitive management styles

■ What Do Your Competitors Offer?

Because it is usually your product that customers will compare to the competition, this is the first thing you should examine. How is your competitor's product different from your own? Put yourself in your customer's shoes and evaluate what you see. Because you need to convince consumers to choose your product over the competition's, you must know what you are up against. You should emphasize the best aspects of your product and what makes it unique.

You can find out about the competition's product by reading their sales literature. This is very important information because it is what the customers are also reading. What impression does the sales literature give you? If you are comparing your product to a competitor's, you can go to a store and actually look at the product. Ask salespeople about it and see what they say. It may or may not be worth it to buy the product, depending on how intimately you want to know it.

■ What's Their Price?

Price is a key aspect of competition. For many consumers, price holds a great deal of sway in their decision to buy. If the competition charges a much lower price than you do, you need to justify that higher price to the customer. Where are your prices generally—high, middle or low? Are you a market leader? (There is a more detailed discussion of price later in this chapter.)

■ Packaging

Examine your competition's packaging, so that you know how to make your product stand out. The way your product is packaged is one of the first impressions a potential customer will get. You want your product to get picked up first, and knowing the competition's packaging will help you make your product stand out. You don't want to create a package that you love and then find out that your main competitor uses the same colors.

■ Where Are They Located?

Where are your competitors located? Does their location have any impact on how they provide their product? Are there any advantages and disadvantages to their location? How does their location impact your company?

Your competitors' locations tell you how much access they have to the market. Location will also tell you what their production and overhead costs probably are. A company located in New York City will pay much higher overhead, including labor costs, than a company located in Omaha. If you are offering a service, is your competitor close to a large customer base?

■ Do They Deliver?

Could delivery and/or installation be relevant to your product? Offering delivery to consumers may be a distinguishing factor that would attract customers to you, especially if the competition does not offer it. If the competition offers delivery and installation, you may have to provide the same service to compete effectively. Again, knowing what your competition is doing will help you place yourself in the market. Think about how you might offer a unique service, like providing a toll-free telephone line that customers can call if they have installation questions.

■ Service and Customer Relations: "How may I help you?"

If service is an essential part of your product, compare your service and customer relations policies to those of your competitors. When customers perceive that a company has excellent customer service, they are loyal to that company's products. Companies with satisfied customers usually command a larger market position than others. You can find how the competition's service and customer relations policies work by visiting their stores or calling them for information.

■ Promotion: "Buy now and..."

This communication by marketers informs, persuades, and reminds buyers of a product to elicit an opinion or response. Knowing what kind of promotional strategies your competitors use can help you to counter them. Do they offer coupons, samples, free trials, or product warranties? What kind of advertising messages do they send to the customer? How effective is that advertising? What media mix do they use to reach their target market? How much do your competitors spend on promotions and how does that amount compare to what you spend? Again, knowing what your competitors are doing to win over potential customers will help you successfully woo them yourself.

■ What Channel Are They On?

Through what channels do your competitors sell their products? If they sell direct, what sales techniques do they use? How does your sales strategy compare? Do you think their sales strategy is effective and has a real impact on their sales volume? You may choose to use the same sales strategies as your competitors if those strategies appear to be the most effective way to reach your target market. You may also choose to try other sales strategies to reach a different target market. Maybe your competitor sells through retail chains, but you believe a large customer base would buy through mail-order. You may then choose to tap into that market instead of competing head-to-head.

■ Are They "Techies"?

In certain industries such as electronics and computers, integrating the latest technology into products is very important. You should be able to charge a premium for providing state-of-the-art technology, if your target customer is informed and sees the value. Are your competitors technologically up-to-date? Do they develop new technologies and implement them? Or are you the leader? If you can't lead, you may want to gear your marketing efforts toward an emphasis that people really don't need the latest and most expensive technology to be successful.

■ How Do They Manage?

Knowing your competitors' management structure will provide a basis for understanding their marketing decisions. Do you think your competitors can make quick and accurate decisions? Do you think they could react quickly to changes you might make in your marketing strategies? In other words, if you launch a new and innovative product, will your competitors adapt their strategies immediately or will you have a significant lag time when you reap the benefits?

Is your competitors' management typically reactionary or does it take an active, directed approach in leading the company? Do you believe your competitors will remain strong in the future?

■ Competition Checklist

✓ Have you compared all aspects of your competitors' products with your own?

✓ Have you examined their packaging?

✓ Have you considered the impact of their location on their business?

✓ What about their delivery and installation policies?

✓ How much do you know about their customer service?

✓ Do you know what their promotional strategies are?

✓ What sales channels and selling techniques do they use?

✓ Are they technologically up-to-date?

✓ What's their management structure? How alert are they to market changes?

■ Review Questions

1. Who are the competitors of Southwest Airlines' business travel fares?

2. What is the first thing you should examine when studying the competition?

3. What is the best way to make your product stand out from the competition?

4. How can knowing about your competitors' locations help you understand the market?

5. What elements of competitive service should be identified?

6. Compare the management structures of a large and a small company and identify how it may impact your marketing efforts.

■ Activities

1. Identify your key competitors (those who offer the same product or service as your firm). Then identify non-key competitors, or those who offer broad product substitutes that may satisfy the same general need or want.

2. Perform a competitive analysis relative to your business. Use the Competition portion of the Market Analysis template (1-MKTANL.DOC).

3. Compare your company to those of your key competitors. Use the Competitive Roundup portion of the Market Analysis template (1-MKTANL.DOC).

Chapter 5

Your Product

If you look at your product critically, as a customer would, you will have a better sense of what you are selling. Would you buy your product if you saw it in a store? Your product should satisfy a need and offer a clear benefit. What psychographic need are you satisfying and how? In profiling your product, you must take a critical look at the product itself.

■ **Product Life Cycle**

Most products have a life cycle that can be broken down into four stages: introduction, growth, maturity, and decline. Each stage of the product's life poses both opportunities and risks. The life cycle does not specifically apply only to your product, but to all the products that directly compete with yours. In other words, your product could enter its life cycle during the maturity phase because other similar products already exist and have brought the product past the introduction and growth phases.

Phase 1: Introduction

The introduction phase can either be the beginning of a whole new industry or the presentation of a new product within an existing industry. In this phase, you try to gain recognition for your product. Customer perceptions, expectations, and preferences are often not yet formed in the introductory phase, and, usually, there is little or no competition. If there are high barriers to entry, meaning that

Learning Objectives

After completing this chapter, you should be able to:
1. Understand strategies throughout the product life cycle
2. Choose a positioning strategy for your product
3. Determine Return on Investment
4. Place your product within a larger scope of product offerings

other companies can't copy your product without large investments, the introduction phase will probably be long. This will affect the marketing strategies you use. You may charge more for your product or you may try to sell as many of your product as possible before competitors can enter the market.

Phase 2: Growth

In the growth stage, sales expand and the product becomes broadly known to the target market. Customers have developed clearer expectations and stronger preferences, and companies try to establish brand loyalty. In the growth stage, companies with new twists on the product enter the market. Competitors look for underserved market segments or weaknesses in your strategy to move in on your customer base. Sometimes, large companies see potential in your product and directly attack your market segment.

In the growth phase, your advertisements will no longer be geared toward creating customer awareness of your product. Instead, you want to differentiate your product from the competition. You may lower prices, especially if you charged higher prices before competitors entered the market. You simply can't maintain those prices after similar and cheaper products enter the market.

Phase 3: Maturity

It is difficult to enter a specific market during the maturity stage because a few strong companies usually dominate the market. They are the ones that survived the growth stage. At this point, customers usually have already developed brand loyalty and are unlikely to try something new. If you have something unique about your product, you might successfully enter the market and gain market share.

One of the marketing strategies that companies use in this stage is to try to get customers to use more of their product. Companies may also try to win over the competition's customers and convert nonusers.

Phase 4: Decline

The final stage of a product's life cycle is characterized by decreasing sales and companies exiting the market. Over their lifetime, most companies have at least several different products, so usually a company will simply withdraw a product from the market when it hits the decline stage and continue to sell its newer products.

The decline stage can mean opportunity for some companies. When a product enters the decline phase, there may not be enough demand to support eight different companies. But demand does not disappear overnight, and one or two companies may find it worthwhile and profitable to keep producing an older product.

Companies that can identify market needs accurately and act rapidly to meet those needs with high-quality goods are the ones that will survive and prosper. A company that is fully committed to meeting customer needs as well as committed to success should have a product portfolio that includes items in various stages of the life cycle. In this way, the company will always have new products ready to take the place of ones entering the declining stage. Your marketing plan needs to reflect your awareness of this.

■ Positioning Your Product

Positioning your product is a key element of the marketing mix. To successfully position your product in the market, you must know what your competitors are doing and differentiate it from other products. Knowing your competitors' niches will help you find one of your own, or at least know how *not* to position your product. Do you want to be known as the "low price leader" or as the "high quality leader?"

■ Return on Investment

Return on Investment (ROI) for your product should be viewed from two different perspectives: your consumer's and your company's. Just as customers weigh several factors (most prominently, getting their money's worth), so, too, should you consider the impact your marketing investments are making on your revenues, the value you bring to your customers, and your profit levels.

Most customers who purchase your product will want a return on their investment. In other words, they want your product to save them time, save them money, make their life easier, or make them feel better. To ensure your customers' satisfaction, you must consider how your product delivers value for the price. What benefit does your product provide the consumer?

The most straightforward approach to ROI is to take the net profit (after taxes) that your product generates and divide it by the total amount invested in product development and marketing. Generally, your ROI will increase over time because you won't need to invest in product development in proportion to your revenues. In fact, you may not have a positive ROI in the short run if your product requires a great deal of investment for development. Determining how long you can wait to recapture your investment is one way to plan.

■ Product Scope

Because most companies have more than one product, it is helpful to place the different products in a bigger picture. Do you have a narrow product line, both high- and low-end products, or a product-service package? Do your competitors have the same setup? It is important to know if your customers want variety to meet their different needs. Customers often want to stick with one brand and will choose the brand that offers them choice.

■ Product Checklist

✓ Have you made an active effort to look at your product from the customer's viewpoint?

✓ Have you thought about where your product is in its product life cycle? Have you considered the life cycle of products that compete with your products, both directly and indirectly?

✓ Have you considered how you want to position your product against the competition?

✓ Have you thought about the benefits that your product provides the customer—the customer's return on his or her investment in your product?

✓ What about the product's ROI for your company—what do you get when you divide your net profit by the amount you have invested in product development and marketing?

✓ Is your product part of a strong product line? What about your competitors' product lines?

■ Review Questions

1. Briefly describe the four stages of the product life cycle.

2. What is product positioning? Why is it important to position against the competition?

3. How does ROI to the customer compare to ROI to the company?

4. Why is it important to look at the scope of your product offerings?

■ Activities

1. Identify the stage of the product life cycle your company's product is in, and identify the stage of the product life your industry is in. Use the Product Life Cycles portion of the Market Analysis template (1-MKTANL.DOC).

2. Draw an X and Y axis, labeling the end points of the X-axis as high and low price and the Y-axis as high and low quality, or some other factors important in differentiating competitive products. Place your product on this positioning grid, and then place your competitors on this grid. Is your product differentiated enough from the competition? Use the Positioning portion of the Marketing Communications template (2-MARCOM.DOC) to assist you.

3. Estimate ROI for your company and your customers. Use the Return on Investment portion of the Market Analysis template (1-MKTANL.DOC).

Chapter 6

Your Price

This chapter contains information on the factors that influence and control the price you charge for your product.

Learning Objectives

After completing this chapter, you should be able to:

1. Understand the production curve of your product or service

2. Identify the price elasticity of your product

3. Choose pricing strategies and tools

■ Production Curve

Your product's production curve tells you how much it costs to produce a certain item at different production levels. Understanding the production curve can help you price intelligently based on the costs you incur at different levels of production. As you might imagine, producing 100 pairs of shoes would be more expensive per pair than producing 25,000 pairs because you made a start-up investment in equipment.

Your goal should be to find that level at which you have the lowest average cost and meet consumer demand. If demand is low for your product and you do not want to overproduce, you may have to produce at a less than optimal level. Therefore, raise your price. Furthermore, if there is excess demand for your product and you have to overproduce to satisfy demand, you may also need to raise the price to pay increased production costs.

■ Price Elasticity

Price elasticity refers to how demand fluctuates as prices change. Demand is usually either elastic or inelastic. Elastic demand means that as you change your price, the amount of goods bought will fluctuate. For example, if you lower your price by $20, you will sell more products, and if you raise the price, you will sell less. Inelastic demand remains relatively constant even when prices change.

Demand for luxury items or specialty products tends to be more elastic than demand for necessities. However, just because demand for toilet paper is inelastic does not mean you can simply raise your price. But if all toilet paper manufacturers raise their prices, demand will probably remain relatively constant.

■ Pricing Strategies

Pricing can be one of the most effective marketing tools you have to promote your product. Price conveys image, affects demand, and helps you target a specific market segment. Your pricing strategies should be consistent with the company's overall goals and objectives. For example, if one of your company goals is to gain a majority market share and sell to a wide cross-section of consumers, you would not want to price your product too high. To choose a pricing strategy, you must look at your target market, your customers, your competitors, and your risks. In a successful business, price must be sufficient to cover total costs while allowing some margin of profit.

Matching the Competition

Using a competitor's prices as a benchmark for pricing your product is a common tactic. In a mature market, you may have to react to your competitors' prices. If you are entering a mature market, make sure that your company can charge the same or less than the competition. You must make sure that the price still makes your company money or at least covers your variable costs. Remember not to charge a competitive price if your product does not deliver the same value for the money as your competitors deliver.

Undercutting the Leader

If you want to gain more market share or penetrate the market, undercut the leader's price. Again, you need to make sure that you can afford to do that and that there is enough demand to absorb your production costs. In some cases, you will want to offer a product of comparable quality for a lower price. If customers are very sensitive to price, even to the point where they will sacrifice quality, undercutting the leader may work for you. Offering a lower-quality product would most likely cost you less and so you could still make a good profit.

If you do try this strategy, though, you should anticipate what the competition will do in response. Could they also afford to cut prices or are they restricted by costs? Would they just have to accept that part of their market is taken? Would they retaliate in another way?

Pricing for Image

Customers often see price as equal to quality—the more you charge, the better your product. A certain image is also often attached to expensive brand names. Customers will, in many cases, pay more for an image. If Armani suits suddenly dropped in price to half of what they now cost, the brand would probably lose much of its prestige.

If you do price for image, you should take that into account in other marketing activities. Your advertising and promotions should also portray that image of exclusivity and quality.

■ Other Price-Related Tools

Regardless of the pricing strategy used, certain promotion tools can affect the frequency and/or the timing of customer buying. These tools can affect how the customer feels about the price of your product without your actually changing the price.

Discounts

Your pricing strategy can include discounts under specific terms. For example, if someone buys more than 20 units of your product, you give them a fifteen percent discount. If they pay immediately, you give them a ten percent discount. It may cost you more to process credit card purchases, so you might charge more, and give a cash discount. Discounts often get the consumer to buy more because they are paying less per product.

One very successful type of discount are frequent-customer programs, such as airlines' frequent-flier programs. If these programs attract or retain more customers, the benefits outweigh the costs. Practically nothing is spent on this incentive for unqualified customers or prospects. The money is spent on existing customer relationships. Often, people will stick with one particular company to get the benefits of discounts or free products/services. The consumer relationship is thus very strong.

Trade-In Allowances

Trade-in allowances are an effective way to lower the final price to the customer without actually lowering the list price. When using this tool, a company allows customers to trade in a used product when they buy a new version of the same. By allowing trade-ins, you are giving the customer the benefit of not having to sell their old product. They may choose you over another company if you provide that convenience.

Coupons

Coupons are another effective way to tailor your pricing strategy to the consumer market. Coupons can be mailed directly to consumers' homes, delivered in local newspapers, or offered in the store where the product is sold. Coupons can also be provided as part of the product package to encourage future buying of the same or other products that you offer. Many cost-conscious consumers shop only for things they can buy with coupons. Coupons can reach a part of the market you wouldn't otherwise reach.

Sales Terms and Credit: "Will that be cash, check, or charge?"

Another way to affect the ultimate price you charge the customer is to use sales terms and credit. Sales terms allow customers to take a discount if they pay their invoice within a specified period of time. A typical discount might be 2/10 net 30. Translated into English, this means the customer can take a two percent discount if the invoice is paid within 10 days. If the invoice is not paid within 10 days, the full amount, without the discount, is due in 30 days.

Freight Pricing Terms

The question of who pays for transportation is an issue. One way to find the best approach is to interview your customers. Following are some pricing terms you should consider:

FOB versus FOB Delivered: With FOB (free on board), the seller is responsible for the cost of loading goods onto the transportation vehicle. At that point, the customer is responsible for all freight charges, the cost of unloading, and any damage that happens during transport. This can be changed to FOB Delivered so that the seller pays all transportation costs and is responsible for any damage that occurs until the buyer takes physical possession of the goods.

Customers like to think they are getting something for free, and offering FOB Delivered is one way to give them that impression. You need to consider how much you can mark up your price to cover your cost of delivery. If offering FOB Delivered terms increases the number of orders you get, the gains may outweigh the risks.

Uniform Standard Price: You can offer a standard price for all shipments, regardless of where you ship your product. One advantage of this approach is that customers know exactly what they are paying. Customers who live near you, however, may feel that they should not have to pay as much to receive your product as someone on the other side of the country.

Zone Pricing: Zone pricing takes care of the distance issue. If you decide to use this approach, you need to establish a number of geographic zones. Then, you establish a shipping price for people in each different zone. Customers are likely to view this as a fair way of pricing.

Freight Absorption: Freight absorption means that you pay the price of shipping your product. If you believe customers will be much more likely to buy your product if shipping charges are included, it may be worthwhile to take this approach. You can also try to incorporate the cost of shipping in to your price so that, while customers think shipping is free, they are in fact paying for all or part of it.

■ Pricing Checklist

✓ Have you studied your production curve closely enough to know the level at which you have the lowest average cost *and* can meet customer demand?

✓ How does the price of your product affect demand?

✓ Have you considered all the pricing strategies that apply to your product? Have you developed your strategy?

✓ Have you considered ways to offset the price of your product, for example, with discounts or coupons?

✓ What are your sales terms and credit terms?

■ Review Questions

1. What is a production curve? What is the primary goal of the production curve?

2. Describe three different options for pricing strategies.

3. What are some pricing tools that offer price reductions to customers?

4. What are some pricing tools that allow payment options to customers?

■ Activities

1. Determine the production curve for your company. Use the Pricing portion of the Market Analysis template (1-MKTANL.DOC).

2. Estimate the price elasticity of your product in response to price changes. Use the Pricing portion of the Market Analysis template (1-MKTANL.DOC).

3. Identify the pricing strategy used by your firm. Use the Pricing portion of the Market Analysis template (1-MKTANL.DOC).

4. Set pricing policies regarding discounts and payment terms. Use the Pricing portion of the Market Analysis template (1-MKTANL.DOC).

Chapter 7

Your Risks

By the nature of competitive markets, risk always exists in a business environment; every business must contend with it. The purpose of this chapter is to identify as many possible sources of your risk so that you are prepared.

No one can anticipate all types of risk, but it is worthwhile to analyze those you do see. An excellent way to reduce risk is to diversify. If you sell several products, your company won't depend on the success of only one product. If you have multiple suppliers, and one goes out of business or starts selling exclusively to your competition, you will not be left helpless. You can also greatly diminish certain risks by purchasing insurance for things such as fire, theft, and illness.

The key is not to avoid risk, but to anticipate and minimize the negative effects of potentially risky activities.

 **Learning Objectives**

After completing this chapter, you should be able to:

1. Identify direct risks to your business

2. Identify environmental risks

■ Business Risks

The first and perhaps the largest business risk you will encounter is the cost structure of your industry, which determines the amount of capital and fixed assets you need to operate your business. The type of business you are in will dictate how much money you need to invest and how risky your venture will be. If you enter an industry that requires a great deal of infrastructure and manufacturing capability, your initial investment will have to be very large and you stand to lose more if the business fails.

Another type of cost structure risk is the need to expand your facilities. Try to foresee the need to increase production or modernize your facilities as an integral part of your long-term financial strategy. Examine ways you could expand your production capacity without building new capacity from scratch.

Competition and Industry Growth

Competition is a risk for every business. Even if you have a new and innovative product or service that no other company is offering, it is just a matter of time before someone tries to take part of your market away.

You should look at some basic issues to determine the risk of competition. How much investment does a company need to produce your product? The more investment needed to produce your product, the lower the risk of competition. Do you have key experience or technology that would be hard for another company to acquire? Do you have contracts with large-scale buyers? Do you have a strong distribution system? Is the industry expanding sufficiently to support the business of multiple competitors and you?

Product Liability

In this litigious day and age, all companies are vulnerable to lawsuits. For some products, you can control this risk factor by purchasing product liability insurance. The costs of protecting your business from product liability claims should be tied to the cost structure of your industry and market.

Profit Margin

Another type of risk has to do with your profit margin, or the percentage of net profits to sales. Some companies have a very low profit margin but a high volume in sales, while others sell very little and have a high profit margin. The way to minimize the risk of low volume sales is to have extra cash on hand while the company adjusts to the changing market.

Seasonal Business

Most businesses sell more during particular time periods. Some businesses are highly seasonable and need to estimate their inventory and cash needs as the season begins, matures, and closes.

Knowing that this risk exists is the first step to deal with it. The better you know your industry and your past performance, the more likely you will make the right purchasing decisions. The best way to minimize your risk is to be conservative. Order what you think will definitely sell, even during a bad season, and try to get your suppliers to send additional goods if you run out. Although it is better to make a profit and run out of goods than to end up with a huge inventory that nobody wants, it is not that simple. If you run out of inventory, you take the chance that your customers will look elsewhere to satisfy their needs. Once they have switched brands, they may not come back. There is no easy solution to this dilemma, but the better you know your situation, the more successful you will be in handling the risk.

Complementary Industries

Your success may partly depend on how well other related or complementary industries are doing. The best way to diminish this risk is to diversify your business so you don't depend on one industry or sector.

Substitution

Most businesses are vulnerable to substitution, when another product serves as a substitute for your own. In effect, any product that can be substituted for yours, even if it is not exactly the same thing, is a threat. There is very little you can do to reduce the risk of substitution; if you have a successful product, others will try to get in on the act. The best thing is to be prepared and keep an eye on any substitutes that may be introduced to the market. Provide your product in a manner valued by your customers and make adjustments to your product strategies in a timely manner.

Suppliers

There is always a risk when you depend on other companies to supply your product. If you depend on a small number of suppliers, you are vulnerable to their control of your business. Suppliers could raise prices or change their trade terms. Your supplier may have a fire or go bankrupt. The more you depend on one supplier, the more risk you face. Build strong relationships with your primary suppliers and keep scanning your business environment for other suppliers who could become your primary suppliers someday, if necessary.

Customers

Some of the same risks you face with a limited number of suppliers can apply to having a limited number of customers. Having a large number of customers maintains a better balance of power for your company.

Another risk of selling to one or two customers who can dictate prices is that you are vulnerable to any competitors who underbid you. Unless there are high barriers to entry in your industry, a competitor may see that you are the exclusive supplier and try to win all or part of that contract from you. If a competitor supplies a comparable product and charges less, the chain may choose your competitor over you.

Key People

Most businesses have certain key personnel who cannot be replaced easily. The best way to reduce the risk of losing important personnel is to create a good working environment, to pay a fair salary, to offer a contract, or to give these people a stake in the company, possibly through share options. While you cannot guarantee that key people will stay forever, you can improve the chances that they remain by making employee retention a priority in the way you run your business.

■ Environmental Risks

Economics

The general economic situation in a region or country can greatly impact your business. There is very little you can do to eliminate the risk of bad economic times, but you can be aware of them and adjust your marketing strategies to meet the changed market. If you see a recession coming, consider cutting back production, lowering your prices, or changing and intensifying your promotional messages.

Weather

Weather can be a substantial risk to your company. You need to figure out how weather could impact your business. It can affect the supply of raw materials for your products. Weather could also affect what you offer. Weather could also affect your physical business or where you sell. If your building is vulnerable to flooding or earthquakes, you should buy the proper insurance and have alternate disaster plans in place.

Government and Law

There is almost always the risk that a local, state, or federal law will be enacted that affects your business. The best way to reduce that risk is to keep abreast of politics that involve your industry. Certain industries are more vulnerable to government regulation. If you are in a highly regulated industry, it pays to keep informed and avoid problems by adhering to the regulations. Large companies often lobby governments to influence decisions that affect their businesses.

■ Risk Checklist

✓ Have you considered the risks inherent in the cost structure of the industry?

✓ Have you carefully considered the risks you face from the competition?

✓ Have you considered how product liability issues might affect you?

✓ What is your profit margin? Have you taken appropriate steps to protect yourself in case of low sales?

✓ How seasonal is your business? What is your strategy for handling the particular seasonality issues that affect you?

✓ How dependent are you on complementary industries? What steps have you taken to minimize your risk in this area?

✓ How vulnerable is your product to substitution?

✓ How strong is your position in relation to your suppliers? Do you have good relationships? Should you be on the lookout for alternate suppliers?

✓ Are there any risks inherent in your customer base—for example, do you depend on very few customers?

✓ Are you doing everything you can to keep your key personnel?

✓ How alert are you to upcoming changes in the economy?

✓ Everybody talks about the weather. What steps are you taking to do something about it—as it affects your business?

✓ Do you stay abreast of politics and laws that may affect your industry? Do you know and follow the regulations that apply to your business?

■ Review Questions

1. Can one avoid all risk by identifying all risk?

2. List and briefly describe six business risks that should be identified.

3. List and briefly describe three environmental risks to a business.

■ Activities

1. Describe the business risks to your firm. Use the Business Risk portion of the Market Analysis template (1-MKTANL.DOC).

2. Describe the environmental risks to your firm. Use the Environmental Risk portion of the Market Analysis template (1-MKTANL.DOC).

3. Calculate the overall risk to your firm. Use the Elements of Risk table in the Market Analysis template (1-MKTANL.DOC).

Chapter 8

Information Resources

Some of the resources and information you need to carry out your market analysis can be found in your own company. Some companies hire outsiders to carry out their market research. There are two types of sources for doing market research: primary and secondary. Primary resources are people who actually buy your product or people involved in selling it. Secondary resources are documents that provide you with information. Following are some ideas of where and how to get information for your market analysis.

The information in this chapter is to help you conduct your market analysis. There is no specific section about information resources in the Market Analysis worksheet.

Learning Objectives

After completing this chapter, you should be able to:

1. Identify primary resources for undertaking a market analysis

2. Recognize secondary resources for undertaking a market analysis

■ Primary Resources

Look at Your Own Record

You should never overlook your own company as a source of valuable information to incorporate when conducting a market analysis. If you are a start-up company, you will have no information to look at, except past efforts and experiences of individuals. If you are an established company, you should examine your past performance, the company as a whole, and the results of your marketing efforts specifically. Your marketing and sales group, as well as your top management, should identify what has been learned and how future marketing and sales efforts could be improved.

Customers

Your customers are a good source of information because they have considered and decided to buy your product. You can find out information about your customers or by asking them to fill out short surveys, or by requesting their ZIP Code when they make purchases.

If you want more detailed information from your customers, you can organize focus groups. Focus groups are small groups of customers or potential customers who get together to discuss different aspects of your product. A facilitator leads the group so that the discussion addresses issues you want more information about.

You can also speak with customers at trade shows. A common strategy that companies use is to give something free to people if they fill out a questionnaire or information card. Even if you just get business cards, you can later contact those people and conduct interviews over the phone.

Salespeople

Your salespeople are in direct contact with your customers and probably have some insight about what customers like and don't like about your product. Depending on the way your company is structured, you can have regular meetings with your salespeople to solicit ideas and observations or you can conduct surveys or interviews with some of them.

■ Secondary Resources

Trade Publications

A wide variety of trade publications, including magazines and newsletters, offer you a great deal of valuable information. Consider subscribing to them. If you have a very low budget, public libraries often have a wide selection of trade publications.

Competitor Literature

An effective way to find out about your competitors is to get their sales literature and annual reports. You can find this information at trade shows and retail outlets, or you can simply phone and request it.

Periodicals

Newspapers, magazines, and other periodicals can provide valuable information for your market research. Surveying periodicals keeps your market information up-to-date.

Government Sources

The government at all levels publishes large amounts of information about industries, regions, and people. Some common sources are chambers of commerce, Small Business Administration regional offices, and government libraries and fax-back services.

Investor Reports

Investment analysts and firms often publish in-depth reports about industries and businesses that may provide you with valuable information about your industry and competitors.

Online Services

There are many online services that connect you to extensive information. You'll find specific discussion groups about certain industries, trade forums, and news services that help you scan a wide range of publications.

Internal Sources

Don't forget to look at your own company's literature for information. Previous marketing plans, balance sheets, sales figures, and inventory records are among the items that will provide you with important information to complete your market analysis.

■ Information Resources Checklist

✓ Have you taken all the steps you can to ask your customers for information?

✓ Do you regularly solicit ideas and observations from your sales force?

✓ Do you stay current in the trade publications for your industry?

✓ Have you studied your competition's literature?

✓ Do you stay in touch with the larger economy by reading or skimming newspapers and magazines?

✓ Have you taken advantage of information you can get from different levels of government and civic organizations?

✓ Have you considered getting an investor report about your industry?

✓ Do you get information from the online services that are now available?

■ Review Questions

1. What are the three primary sources of information needed to understand the market?

2. What are secondary sources available to you to perform your market analysis?

■ Activities

1. List internal company records you could collect to help you with market analysis.

2. How can you get information or feedback from your customers? Is marketing research needed?

3. Define ways to get information or feedback from your sales force.

4. List secondary sources of information available to you in your library or online.

1-MKTANL.DOC

The Market Definition section describes the existing and projected marketplace in which you will introduce your company and products.

Consult industry analysts, census reports, and trade journal studies for this information.

Market Definition

Industry Analysis

The _____ market is growing at a rapid rate. The market for these products amounted to $_____ million in 19_____ — representing a _____% growth over $_____ million in 19_____ .

Referenced sources agree that the major trends are: _____

_____

_____ .

The overall _____ market for the _____ industry is projected to be

$_____ [*million/billion*]_____ by the end of 19_____ . The overall market potential for [*product category*]_____

is estimated to be $_____ million by 19_____ , and the [*additional products*]

_____ portion of this market

is estimated to be $_____ million.

The area of greatest growth in the _____

market is in the area of _____ .

You can define the market segment by product feature, by lifestyle of target customers, by geographical location, by season, etc.

How is the market distributed among major participants?

What are the share gain and loss trends?

Summarize your view of the trends and implied opportunities.

For an existing business (your own or a recent acquisition), review sales history, market share and position, industry trends, profits, marketing methods.

What do industry forecasters predict for the next two years?

Market Segment

Key points in defining the market segment for [*product*] _____

are _____ ,

_____ .

Currently, the market is shared by _____ participants.

Users of [*product*] _____
are looking for _____

The stability of this market segment is [*volatile, uncertain, solid, etc.*] _____

_____ , based on _____

product category performance over the past two years.

By broad category, list the types of customers you are likely to sell to (e.g., retailers, electrical contractors, mail-order catalogs, etc.).

Consult industry analysts, census reports, and trade journal studies for this information.

Repeat the information about market segments for as many segments as are required.

The major market segments are:

[Segment 1] _____

and [Segment 2]_____ .

The _____ segment of the market is generally based on [products] _____ with retail prices in the range of $_____ to $_____ . The vast majority of sales in this category will be handled by [OEMs/retailers/manufacturer's representatives/direct channels/etc.] _____ .

Over the past _____ years, [similar product manufacturers or service providers] _____ companies have proven that meaningful features can be developed for this class of [product]_____ : _____ , _____ and _____ . These companies have primarily focused on the use of [manufacturing technique/special materials/recipes/chemicals/machinery/etc.] _____ _____ to improve the quality of _____ in a [product]_____ . These products have been successfully distributed in many areas of the industry. Competitive products in this market are [produced/provided] _____ by [competitor 1] _____ , [competitor 2] _____ , and [competitor 3] _____ .

In the next _____ to _____ years, it is estimated that there will be more than _____ [thousand/million] _____ of [products] _____ distributed by [Company] _____ . The market potential for [product] _____ in these quantities—with a current retail price of $_____ per unit—is approximately $_____ million. This translates to a market share of _____ % of the overall market.

Of the _____ customers, approximately _____ % will [buy/use/want/expect] _____ [product] _____ to help them to [*deliver their work/maintain x/expedite their production/reduce costs/ etc.*]_____.

_____ of these [*products*] _____ will have a _____ capability, and about _____

of those [*products*] _____ will require [*other features*]_____.

You might also consider how else the product/service is favorably differentiated from the competition: in actual performance, in quality and reliability, in production efficiencies, in breadth of line and/or options.

When determining your most powerful assets, include those in segmentation, distribution, pricing, and awareness/image.

Consider your corporate strengths, including size, financial resources, people, reputation and business relationships.

Strengths

In terms of product strength, [*product*] _____
has several distinct advantages over the competition.

In marketing, our most powerful assets are _____

_____

_____

_____.

In the corporate arena, [*Company*] _____
is supported by _____

_____

_____

_____

_____.

Weaknesses

There [*is/are*] _____ [*no/two/etc.*] _____ handicaps inherent in our product. The only notable marketplace disadvantages are _____

_____

and those are because [*explanation*] _____

_____

_____

_____.

By 19_____, we should be able to position ourselves in order to _____

_____

and thereby reduce this weakness considerably.

Corporate weaknesses, at this time, consist only of .... However, we are taking steps

to .... ,

which we feel should alleviate this problem.

Opportunities

The upside potential for [our products].. in

[each of the currently addressed markets] ....

Can the current line of products and technological capabilities be leveraged effectively?

over the next two years is ....

What is the estimated cost of entry, timeframe, and risk?

An altogether new application for this product would be tapping .... markets.

Further opportunity for our product exists in .... market(s).

Examples of other possibilities for development include alternative distribution, technology licensing, creating up/down market brands, etc.

Still another possibility for development involves ....

Identify threats to your company from both internal and external sources.

Internal threats: computer sabotage by a disgruntled employee, computer virus, etc.

Threats

Internal Threats

Internal threats to our company include ....

External threats: attempted hostile takeover, price war, etc.

External Threats

External environmental threats to our company include ....

Do you require immediate preventive action? If yes, what is that action, and when does it need to be performed?

Preventive Action to be Taken

In order to deal with the threats described above, the following preventive actions will be taken:

[*Preventive action 1*] ....

by [*timeframe, e.g., 3 months*] ....

[*Preventive action 2*] ....

by [*timeframe*] ....

Consider customer demographics (age, income, sex, family, location, and occupation) and psychographics (lifestyle, motives, needs, interests, and purchase history).

Customer profile: innovator, early adopter, early majority, late majority, or laggard?

Customer Profile

The most typical customer for our product is someone who is (specify demographics and psychographics), and who currently uses [*product*] .... for [*application/purpose*] ....

Who influences the final decision to purchase?

What current economic factors influence your customer's spending?

Our customers are influenced by ....

....

Our customers are located (geographics) ....

and purchase by (biographics) ....

Ask your customers what motivates them to buy your product.

It is easy to understand why the people are motivated to buy ....

because ....

....

On a separate page in your marketing plan, list your major existing customers alphabetically. If appropriate, state their application of your product.

Customer List

....

....

....

How are the key competitors perceived?

Consider size, ability to finance future growth, name recognition, experience in field, expertise or core competencies in specific disciplines, rapid response to market changes and challenges.

Consider the same characteristics for weaknesses.

How is this competitor positioning itself in the market?

What markets is this competitor pursuing? How?

What strategies should you pursue to increase business against this competitor?

How will you respond to this competitor's strengths and weaknesses?

Do they have a competitive advantage? How?

Do these identified advantages present a barrier to entry into the market?

Provide recommendations for positioning your product against this competitor. Consider channels of distribution, price, packaging, promotion, customer appeal and loyalty, and other factors.

Discuss your key competitors with regard to product or service, price, location, promotion, management, financial position.

Look in the Yellow Pages.

Look in the industrial directories at your local library. Search online databases that provide competitive profiles of other companies.

Competition

Our main competitor's strengths are ....

Our main competitor's weaknesses include ....

This competitor's strategy is ....

We will respond to this competitor by ....

We will position [*product*] .... against this competitor by ....

[*Company's*] .... product(s) offer .... in .... situations.

Read industry magazines; look for advertisers.

False or incomplete information here translates as dishonesty and negligence to investors, bankers, etc.

Do not delude yourself (or your investors) about the competition.

If you are well-known in your industry, survey your competitor's order line anonymously and ask how their products are better than yours.

Companies that compete in this market are [competitor 1] _____ , [competitor 2] _____ , and [competitor 3] _____ .

All companies mentioned charge competitive prices [list examples and range of prices] _____
_____

The major strengths and weaknesses of our competitors are [price/location/quality, etc.] _____
_____

The major competitors' objectives and strategies are _____
_____
_____

The major competitors' most likely response to current [economic/social/culture/demographics/geographics/political/governmental/technological/competitive trends] _____
_____

affecting our industry will be [list response of competitors] _____
_____
_____

Our products or services are positioned relative to our major competitors by [price/delivery/location/etc.] _____
_____

New firms entering and old firms leaving this industry affect our product [list how this affects your product] _____
_____

Key factors of [list top factors] _____
_____

have resulted in the present competitive position in this industry.

The nature of supplier and distributor relationship in this industry is [*the supplier and distributor effect on your product*] ....

Competitive threats today come from [*other companies or industries/new or entrenched technologies/foreign countries, etc.*] ....

and ....

Include all comparisons and test results as attachments to your completed marketing plan.

In all comparisons, [*Company's*] .... products provide more features and have superior performance than do competitive products. In most cases, the number of differences is substantial. A complete technical comparison is available.

[*Competitor's*] .... [*competitive*] .... product does not provide the same capabilities in a situation where [*describe circumstances*] ....

This is the only way [*your product*] .... and [*their product*] .... compete.

Competitive Roundup

The following chart illustrates how [*Company's*] .... product compares to the competition in several different key areas.

Rank: 1=Weak to 5=Strong

Use this chart to perform an in-depth analysis of your major competitors.

Columns have been provided to describe your company and two competitors. Add more columns if needed.

Competitive Roundup – Company

Product			
Company			
Estimated 19____ Sales $	$ ____	$ ____	$ ____
Estimated Share of Market	____ %	____ %	____ %
Estimated Advertising Budget	$ ____	$ ____	$ ____

Product Line ....

Quality ....

Technology ....

Advertising Effectiveness ....

Sales Force Excellence ....

Distribution ....

Manufacturing Efficiency ....

Standing in Industry ....

Future Potential ....

Seriousness of Competition ....

Number of Employees ....

Greatest Strength ....

Key Weakness ....

Competitive Roundup – Product

Price ....

Size ....

Capacity ....

Ease of Use ....

Installation ....

Range ....

Appearance ....

Quality ....

Design ....

Useful Life ....

Trade-in Value ....

Technology ....

Responsiveness ....

State-of-the-Art ....

24-Hour Availability/Support ....

Technical Expertise ....

Repair Service ....

Efficiency

Guarantee/Warranty

Complete

On-Time Capability

Upgrades

Have you overlooked market niche opportunities?

Are your resources being deployed against the most serious competitors?

If significant, include competitors' advertisements and brochures as attachments (or have them available upon request).

Observations and Conclusions

It appears, from the above information, that _____

_____

_____

_____

_____ .

Explain life cycle of product/service. Is it in the introduction, growth, maturity, or decline stage?

Create a simple chart covering the life cycles of your products/services. If several products are in different life cycle positions, indicate each separately on the chart.

Product Life Cycles

The life cycle for [product line] _____

can best be described as follows: [describe life cycle position] _____

_____

_____

_____ .

[Product 1] _____ ,

due to our recent efforts to _____ ,

is in a strong position. We feel that for the next [period] _____

What conclusions do you draw from the life cycle positions? Are they up to date? Are there any early warnings of obsolescence?

it will continue to _____

_____

and generate profits at or above expected levels.

[Product 2] _____

will need to be [improved/upgraded] _____ within _____

[months/years] _____ in order to insure that it does not move into its

decline stage.

Overall, we conclude that our products will continue to be viable in the

marketplace during the next _____ [months/years] _____ and that

[Company's] _____ future planning and product-related activities will ensure a strong market presence.

ROI possibilities: fewer rejects or breakdowns, faster turnover of inventory, improved efficiency, improved convenience, lower warranty costs, advantages of a better-quality end product, advantages in cost savings in other areas.

Return on Investment

For most customers, [product] _____ will pay for itself in terms of _____ .

within _____ months, because of _____

Possible savings areas: reduced labor costs, lowered reject rate, reduced downtime, lowered inventory costs, improved convenience, displaced employee activity.

Regarding cost savings, [product] _____ will save our customers money in terms of _____ .

Examples of generating profit include heightened productivity, improved product performance, increased capacity, and concentration on their own business.

Our customers can generate more profits in terms of _____ .

For [Company] _____ , our [product/product line] _____ has shown, and is showing, a positive return on the investment that has been made. [Product/product line] _____ has shown a _____ % ROI during the last [period] _____ , based on net profits divided by the total investment made.

How do you set prices? Is there a policy?
Is your pricing competitive?
Is there perceived value (it costs more, therefore it must be better) inherent in higher prices?
Are prices based on costs (standard markup)?
Why are they higher or lower than competing prices?
How elastic (effect of pricing on demand) is the market for these products? How does consumer preference affect elasticity?

Pricing

The prices for our products are determined first and foremost by [competition/costs/suppliers/manufacturers/package deals] _____ .

It is important to know that [sliding scales/volume/regulated/competitive/perceived value] _____ pricing is essential to our market profile.

List examples of competitive pricing.

Include price comparisons and reports as attachments.

Compared to the competition, our prices are _____.

Different seasonal aspects of our market affect our pricing because [*example: selling seasons*] _____

_____.

We feel that our customers will pay $ _____ because [*purchasing rationale*] _____

_____.

We will be using the following pricing strategies: _____

_____

_____.

Risk

Business Risk

Cost Structure

[*Company*] _____ opened a _____

in [*month/year*] _____. This new [*facility/division*] _____

doubled our capacity and increased our potential capacity by a factor of

_____. In conjunction with this expansion, [*Company*] _____

significantly increased our marketing expense and overhead. Although

[*Company's*] _____ [*products*] _____

were well accepted by the market at former levels of production, there is no

assurance that we will be able to continue successfully marketing our increased

production.

If the market acceptance of our increased production slows, margins and

profitability may suffer. While we operated profitably in the first _____

months ended _____ (unaudited), [*Company*] _____

is unable to predict whether its operating results for the full fiscal year ending

_____ will be profitable.

[*Company*] _____ had planned to add equipment to

further increase production capacity over a period of time from cash flow.

However, market opportunities for [*Company*] _____

products have encouraged us to accelerate our expansion plans. [Company] _____ believes the net proceeds from an [investment/loan] _____ and cash flow from operations will be sufficient to allow [Company] _____ to meet the expected growth in demand for our products. However, there is no minimum investment which must be raised. There can be no assurance that sufficient capital will be raised or that future product sales will meet our growth expectations. Should either of these fail to occur, [Company] _____ may elect to (i) reduce the expansion to a level consistent with our former slower growth plan, or (ii) pursue other financing alternatives. Implementation of either of the foregoing options could delay or diminish [Company's] _____ growth and adversely affect our profitability.

Competition

Match your performance expectations to industry conditions and/or explain how and why your operation will be different.

[Company] _____ competes with national [product] _____ companies, several of whom dominate the [product] _____ market, and are based primarily in [list states] _____.

[Company] _____ and [Company] _____ have greater sales and greater financial, production, distribution, and marketing resources than [Company] _____. Although we believe that in [state] _____ most of the our market share has come from displacement of the brands of the _____ companies, there can be no assurance that competition in the future will not increase from the national brands or from present or new regionally-based [product] _____ companies, many of which, like [Company] _____, have recently completed or are planning significant [facility/capacity] _____ expansions. Furthermore, if the market for [product] _____ continues to grow, the major national [product] _____ companies will likely devote greater resources to this segment.

Industry Growth

The sale and consumption of [product] _____ has increased dramatically over the past _____ years and [Company] _____ and other [product makers/providers] _____ are increasing their capacity in order to meet this growth. There can be no assurance, however, that the growth will continue at the present rate, or at all, and the demand for [product] _____ may not keep up with increases in supply, in which case [Company] _____ may face heightened competition and be unable to sell sufficient quantities of our product to maintain our volume and profit margin.

Product Liability

[Company] _____ has _____ Liability Insurance and will continue such coverage if available at a reasonable cost. However, future increases in insurance premiums could make it prohibitive for us to maintain adequate insurance coverage. A large damage award against [Company] _____ , not adequately covered by insurance, would adversely affect our financial position.

Other business risks include profit margin, seasonality, volatility of industry, substitution, limited suppliers, dependence on major customer, and the performance of your management team.

Other risks include: _____

_____

_____ .

Environmental Risk

Economic

The economic risks affecting [Company] _____ are

_____ .

The best strategy for [Company] _____ is [diversification, offering numerous products or services to multiple market segments] _____

_____ .

Weather

[Company] _____ has provided [planning/

good management/x insurance coverage] _____ to protect against catastrophic weather, such as fire, floods, or drought. Despite these precautions, a major natural disaster could affect our business by causing

_____ .

Legal and Government

The State and Local ordinances or zoning laws that may impact our product are

_____

_____ .

[Company] _____ will stay abreast of legal issues facing *[industry]* _____ through *[industry publications]* _____

and _____

_____ .

This table shows an example of how risk may be evaluated, where it stems from, and which areas are most dangerous. It allows you to compare your exposure, given various assumptions. Modify this list as needed for your product.

The total Overall Risk should always equal 100%.

Assign degrees of risk to each area: low=1, medium=5, high=10. Next, assign a risk weight to each area: 0% – 100%. The total in this column must not exceed 100%. Finally, multiply the degree of risk factor times the weight percentage to calculate the total risk.

Elements of Risk

	Degree of Risk	Weight in %	Total
Business Risk			
Cost Structure			
Competition			
Industry Growth			
Product Liability			
Profit Margin			
Seasonality			
Complementary Industry			
Substitution			
Suppliers			
Customers			
Personnel and Management			

Environmental Risk

Economic

Weather

Legal and Governmental

Overall Risk   100%

In this section, list information to support your risk assumptions. The elements of risk with the highest totals should receive the most explanation.

Rationale

Part 2: Marketing Communications

Marketing communications is the way you communicate with your market. Your marketing communications plan is a key part of your marketing plan because it sets out ways you'll let potential customers know about your product. In Part 1, you analyzed the market you're working in.

What you found out will now be applied to your marketing communications plan to come up with the best approach to successfully reach and sell to your designated market. Chapters 9 through 15 discuss the various aspects of marketing communications.

Chapter 9

Promotion

Promotion is a broad category. Commercials, print ads, billboards, event sponsorships, telephone sales, direct mail, and other promotional devices define and sculpt the company's face and image. The task of the company is to be as clever as possible in how it draws its own face. Remember, hundreds of other faces crowd the market in search of the consumer's dollar!

The purpose of promotion is to tell potential customers that your product can satisfy their needs, to convince those potential customers to buy from you, and to successfully compete with other similar businesses. Your message will depend on the target market you identify and how the market will perceive your message. Thus, the goals of promotion are to inform, persuade, remind, and communicate.

Customers must know that your product exists before they can buy it. A company that is offering a completely new product should develop its message to inform potential customers that the product now exists. In a mature market, a company might aim to let potential customers know that its product is on the market, while also attempting to convince them to buy their product over the competition's. A company with a strong, positive image may only need to keep reminding customers of the products it offers. Once customers remember what that company offers, they will choose it over competitive products. The promotional strategy you choose will be determined by marketing strategy decisions you have already made.

 **Learning Objectives**

After completing this chapter, you should be able to:

1. Understand the goals of promotion

2. Identify key factors that influence marketing communications

3. State marketing communications objectives

4. Budget marketing communications activities

5. Assess marketing communications efforts

■ Know Your Influences

The two key factors that influence the marketing communications directions your company undertakes are your marketing analysis and your budget. Your market analysis will suggest the best mix of marketing communications tools to reach your target market, and your budget will determine the total amount you can or should spend on marketing communications.

■ What Are Your Objectives?

Before you can decide on what mix of marketing communications ingredients to use, you must analyze what your objectives are. If you're offering a new product that no one has heard of, your objective should be to inform as many potential customers as you can of the existence of the product and its benefits. If you're the first to offer the product, you won't have to differentiate yourself from the competition, because you have none.

If you're entering a mature market, however, you should aim to inform customers that your product exists and convince them they should try your product over the competition's. In this case, look at what the competition is doing to promote their product, and then decide how you can make your product stand out. In a mature market, you might try to convince customers to increase usage of your product or to use it for different purposes. At this stage of a product's life cycle, you need to be creative and find new uses for your product. Consumers may not know they have those needs, so your goal is to find and create them and then convince consumers that your product is indeed needed.

In coming up with marketing communications objectives, remember to be realistic. Once you have decided what your objectives are, you can gear your efforts toward reaching them. If you understand what you're trying to achieve, you'll be better prepared to get what you want, and you'll have a yardstick to measure your campaign's success.

Some companies forget how important retaining customers is. Offer only what you can deliver. If you offer more than you can deliver and customers become disillusioned, you won't retain them and will lose future sales from that customer. Nothing kills a good product faster than bad promotion!

■ Budget Your Activities

Depending on where in the product life cycle your product is, you'll spend different amounts to promote your product. If you're launching a new product, you may need a larger budget to successfully place your product on the market. In the introductory phase, you would need to tie your budget closely to forecasted sales.

You'll probably have an overall budget, which you'll then divide into the different promotional areas you decide to use. There's no standard rule to guide allocating your dollars among the different elements of the marketing mix. It will vary greatly in different companies and the types of products they sell.

Spend the money you budget wisely and don't assume that more is better. If your product has a solid presence on the market, spending a lot of money on promotion may have only a slight impact on increasing sales. If your market share is high, to increase that share by a few percentage points may not be a wise expenditure. Think about using the extra dollars to reach a *different* audience. Always compare your investment to the results and decide whether you should continue to allocate funds in the same manner or change your strategy.

However, be aware that measuring results of marketing activities is part science and part art. Attributing specific results directly to specific activities of marketing isn't always accurate or possible. You may need to make subjective calls about the relative effectiveness of individual marketing activities. At times like this, you should go with your "gut feeling." Your experience in this area will serve you well.

The methods outlined below can also be used to set budgets for specific areas, such as advertising or public relations.

Marginal Spending

With the marginal spending approach, you spend on the next promotion an amount equal to the profit generated by the last promotion. If your last advertisement brought about $50,000 in net profit, you would spend that $50,000 on your next ad campaign.

The difficulty in this approach is determining exactly what your profits were. Presumably, you have other marketing activities going on at the time, such as personal selling or public relations, and it's difficult to know exactly how much of your sales can be attributed to a specific promotional activity.

Spending Available Funds

The available funds approach entails spending what you can afford. Although probably the most commonly used method for many businesses, available funds spending is the most conservative and shortsighted. The more you can spend on an effective promotion, the more sales you tend to generate. In other words, if you make an investment in quality advertising, you should generate at least enough revenue to pay for it and contribute to additional revenue and profit.

Before you decide to use this approach, try to estimate how much of an increase in sales you could generate by increasing your promotional budget. You may find it worthwhile to spend more so that your sales will go up. If you're very conservative and spend very little on your marketing communications efforts, your sales may not grow very well. You should look at your marketing communications budget as an investment and fixed cost, not as a luxury item.

Budgetary Spending

In the budgetary spending method, you spend a fixed percentage of projected sales on promotion. If you want sales to reach a certain level next year, you need to spend a certain percentage on promotion during the year.

You take a certain risk with this approach, because there's always the chance that you won't reach your projected sales goals while you're already spending at the higher levels of the forecast. If you're an established company, look at how the past efforts have helped your sales increase. If you're a new company with no track record, you'll either have to feel confident that your projections are reasonable and obtainable or you should use another budgeting method.

The Task Approach

With this method, a company simply decides what "task" they want to perform and budgets the amount of money needed to do it. You might have to eliminate some projects, take money out of cash flow, or go to your bank and borrow the money to do the project.

Match Dollar for Dollar

Another approach is to match dollar for dollar what the competition is spending. This method is based on the assumption that equal spending will at least keep you and the competition equal in sales and market share. Another assumption is that you *know* what the competition is spending.

If you have many competitors, you would probably want to spend the same as the market leader, or, if that's you, what your closest competitor is spending. Some companies spend an average of what their main competitors are spending. This may not be wise if the market leader has a huge budget and a smaller competitor has a tiny budget that keeps the average down. Another problem with this method is determining how much your competitors are spending. Many industries have research data available that calculates spending by company. Your local trade association may have that data, so check with them first.

If you decide to use this approach, remember that equal spending does not necessarily mean that you'll be as successful as your competitor. Simply spending the same amount of money is no guarantee. You should try to make the most out of every dollar you spend—even million-dollar ad campaigns can flop. Success is not found in how much you spend; it will come only if you know who your target market is and find effective methods to convince customers that your product will provide the desired benefits.

■ Track Your Efforts

It's important to remember that over time you'll get better at marketing communications. Devise some method to track the effectiveness of all your promotion activities. As we go through the different areas of marketing communications, we will give some ideas of how you can track performance using different tools. This way, as you create new plans and campaigns, you'll have the tangible evidence to learn from the past and be even more effective in the future.

Now that you have determined what you want to achieve and how much money you have to spend, let's explore the different marketing communications options available to you.

■ Promotion Checklist

✓ Have you analyzed your market? Your market analysis will suggest the best mix of marketing communications tools to reach your target market.

✓ Have you established a marketing communications budget?

✓ Have you set objectives for your marketing communications efforts? What are you trying to accomplish?

✓ Have you determined the best promotion mix? What method will you use to allocate your marketing communications budget?

✓ How are you going to track the effectiveness of your individual marketing communications activities?

■ Review Questions

1. What are the goals of promotion?

2. Discuss how the budget and the market analysis influence your marketing communications programs.

3. Name possible marketing communications objectives throughout the stages of the product life cycle.

4. Briefly describe at least three ways to determine a marketing communications budget.

5. Why is it important that you track your marketing communications efforts?

■ Activities

1. List your objective(s) for marketing communications.

2. Set up your marketing communications budget.

3. Devise methods of tracking the effectiveness of your marketing communications activities.

Chapter 10

Sales Promotions

Sales promotions supplement advertising, public relations, and personal selling. The objective of your sales promotions should be to activate new prospects and bring about sales. Sales promotions serve to push people to take action and to buy now, and can be a particularly effective way to jump-start sales of a new product. (In contrast, advertising and public relations are more involved in putting the notion to buy into consumers' heads.)

 **Learning Objectives**

After completing this chapter, you should be able to:

1. Decide which sales promotions tools to use

2. Delineate sales promotions objectives

3. Devise sales promotions strategies

4. Plan the sales promotions budget

Sales promotion activities come in many forms, depending on the target. For example, sales promotions to final consumers could be banners, aisle displays, samples, calendars, point-of-purchase (POP) displays, coupons, contests, trade shows, rebates, or trading stamps. Sales promotions to intermediaries include price promotions, sales contests, calendars, gifts, trade shows, meetings, and catalogs. You can also target sales promotion to the sales force in the form of contests, bonuses, travel, meetings, displays, sales aids, and training materials.

Be careful that customers don't rely on sales promotions. Some people will buy only when you offer a coupon, and in effect you have just dropped the price of your product.

It's a wise practice to test a potential sales promotion if you can. Start on a small scale to a limited audience. Then, measure the effectiveness to determine whether to expand, adjust, or abandon the promotion. If the response to your promotion is too good, the costs of giveaway items could make the promotion a money loser even though sales have gone up dramatically.

■ Lay Out Your Objectives

It's wise to lay out a series of specific sales promotion objectives so you can measure success. The objectives you choose may also have an effect on the types of sales promotions you choose. For example, if your objective is to promote a greater understanding of your product by potential customers, you might choose to send out samples or set up demonstrations. If you hope to increase sales in the short term and your product already has a strong market presence, you may decide to offer coupons.

Once you have laid out your objectives, you can decide which specific sales promotions will best serve your purposes. Think about the specific purpose of each activity you undertake and what the most effective way will be to track that promotion. Look at what strategies your competitors are using. Are they successful?

Different types of sales promotions will be more or less effective with different target groups. Based on what you know about your target market, you should use the sales promotions that are likely to cause customers to buy. Over time, you'll learn to gauge what prompts your customers to buy.

■ Devise Your Strategies

To make sales promotions work for you, there are a few things you should keep in mind.

Deadline

It's a good idea to put a deadline on sales promotions. You should give the customer a specific timeframe in which to make the purchase. Giving a deadline also makes the promotion appear to be even more of a good opportunity. Often, 60 to 90 days gives customers the incentive to buy now with a reasonable time to act on your offer. Another reason to put a specific end to your sales promotions is that it will help you track the results of your efforts.

Referral

Word of mouth is one of the best ways to market your product. How can you get your customers to speak highly of your product and encourage others to purchase it? Offer incentives to your customers to get recommendations for other potential customers.

Trial

Free trials let customers try your product before they make any investment. If you decide to offer free trials, make sure they are easy to understand. If your free trial is easy, self-explanatory, and really beneficial, you may just get consumers hooked on your product or service.

Remember that people often don't value what they don't pay for. Be sure that you give just enough to provide them a taste of your product and what it offers, but don't give away too much or they won't appreciate it enough to pay for it later.

Feedback

It's imperative that you track your efforts to gauge past performance. If you send out coupons, put source codes on them that tell you where the person lives who used the coupon lives so that you can find out if it's worthwhile to do mailings in a particular geographical area. If you provide a rebate card with your product, you should get the name, address, and telephone number of the person receiving the rebate, as well as the store where they made the purchase. The more information you collect, the better you'll be able to gauge which sales promotions work for your company and which do not.

■ Plan Your Sales Promotion Budget

Sales promotions are an important part of your marketing mix and you must allocate sufficient funds to make them succeed. If your sales promotions are successful, they should more than pay for themselves and bring in new customers, too.

Distributors and retailers generally require you to commit some promotional dollars to their operations to help them sell your product. Being creative and flexible will likely garner the best results. Find out what promotions they have planned and ask them about past performance of these sales promotions. Ask to see the specifics of their promotions in advance. Most importantly, hold distributors and retailers accountable for the results of their promotions that you are helping to fund. Asking questions and demanding accountability are wise business practices.

It's to your benefit to allocate money to your channel distributors' efforts if they help increase your sales. Spend wisely. Often, your channel marketers are more in touch with the market than you are, so listen to what they have to say. And conversely, your in-house marketers may be able to outperform the promotions of your channel distributors. Learn the facts.

■ Sales Promotions Checklist

✓ In deciding which types of sales promotions to use, have you determined how many sales each promotion is likely to produce?

✓ Have you found a way to test a sales promotion before you roll it out on a wider basis?

✓ Have you established overall objectives for your sales promotions? Have you tied each objective to a specific promotion?

✓ Do you have good strategies for making your sales promotions work? Specifically:

- Make sure every sales promotion has a deadline.

- Consider offering incentives to customers for referrals.

- Consider free trials of your product.
- Use every sales promotion to get feedback from your customers—for example, print a source code on coupons so you can track where the customer got them.

✓ Have you estimated the return on each sales promotion so you can allocate your budget wisely?

✓ Have you done your homework on the distributors and retailers to whom you give promotional money?

■ Review Questions

1. Identify at least three sales promotion tools suitable for each of the following audiences: final consumers, intermediaries (such as wholesalers), and employees (such as an internal salesperson).

2. Why is it important to have sales promotion objectives? Why is feedback important?

3. Discuss why deadlines are necessary for sales promotions.

4. Why are customer referrals so important?

5. Evaluate the use of free trial samples.

6. Why must you budget for sales promotions?

■ Activities

1. Determine your target marketing communications audience, and then choose three different sales promotion tools appropriate to that audience.

2. List the objective(s) of your sales promotion.

3. Estimate a budget for each sales promotion task you chose for your firm. Then estimate the return on each sales promotion.

4. If you have planned any trade shows, use the Trade Show Checklist and Schedule template (TRADECHK.DOC).

Chapter 11

Sales Literature

Learning Objectives

Sales literature is the written material that accompanies, represents, or explains your product to potential customers, be they individual end users or distributors. Sales literature includes data sheets, brochures, pamphlets, return cards, rate cards, and form letters—any printed material that helps close a sale.

After completing this chapter, you should be able to:

1. Understand what comprises sales literature

2. Construct a data sheet or product slick

3. Design a brochure

4. Produce a rate card

5. Create form letters

6. Plan a sales literature budget

You should have sales literature prepared before you launch your product so that as soon as inquiries come in, you can supply well thought-out information in a professional style. In all your sales literature, try to remain as consistent as possible. In other words, use your logo and name on everything, and choose a style that will work well in different formats. To generate an image for your business, you must be consistent.

■ Write Your Data Sheets

A data sheet, or product slick as they are sometimes called, provides a detailed look at one specific product on one sheet of paper. As with all sales literature, different companies will use different approaches to the design and text of data sheets. You must know who your audience is and what you're trying to communicate. Data sheets usually include a photo of the product. This can be especially important if the product is new or visually appealing and you want customers to recognize it. Many high-tech or manufacturing firms have detailed data sheets with enough space to properly explain the product's specifications and benefits.

Your data sheets may or may not include the product price. If pricing is a key marketing strategy for you, you would most probably want to include the price. If you're focusing more on quality and durability and your product is priced higher than your competition's, then you may not want to include the price. Instead, you would include an 800 phone number for customers to call for more information. And once you have someone on the phone, you have a much better chance of convincing them to buy.

You can target your data sheets to end user consumers, as the above examples imply, but you can also target distributors. Data sheets can serve as tools to help your distributors and their salespeople to better understand the product they are selling. A salesperson can also use data sheets to back up explanations to the customer and to give the customer something concrete to take home. In that sense, they can serve as a valuable reminder of the relative merits of your product.

■ Design Your Brochures

Brochures are the most common way to get information across about your company and what it does. You may decide that you need several different brochures, depending on who you're sending them to, what you're trying to accomplish, and what your message to the reader is. It is a good idea to come up with a standard brochure about your company, a company profile that includes facts about the company, its vision or mission, its operations, and its products and services. This type of brochure could be used as background material for press, customers, and even potential investors.

You may also design a brochure to highlight one specific product line or service package. You may want to design your brochure with a pocket to hold price lists, data sheets, PR releases, or pictures of new products. A good rule of thumb is that the more expensive or expansive your product is, the longer and more detailed your brochure should be.

■ Sketch Your Rate Cards

For a service business, a rate card provides the potential customer with a list of the rates you charge for different services. A rate card is a reference tool for the customer. The rate card should supplement your brochure and have some introduction to your company and its services. In designing the rate card, keep in mind that you want people to keep it in their files. A stronger bond paper, like card stock, would be appropriate. Remember, the menu in a restaurant is a rate card too, so it should be well designed and easy to read.

■ Create Your Form Letters

It's an excellent idea to create a number of form letters well ahead of any promotion so you respond quickly to queries, with consistency in the messages that you mail or fax to prospective customers. You might create a form letter that thanks the customer for choosing to use your service, for example. As soon as someone becomes a customer, you send them a form letter thanking them for their patronage.

Maybe you create a form letter that responds to customer complaints. That letter might simply say: "Thank you for taking the time to write us with your comment. We are looking into the matter and will contact you soon." If you have the form letter ready, you'll be able to respond quickly and effectively. If you don't have a letter ready, someone will need to draft a letter, get it approved, and then mail it out. This can be a long process that leaves an increasingly dissatisfied customer waiting to hear back from you!

■ Plan Your Sales Literature Budget

The amount of money you should allocate for sales literature is tied to the price of your product. If your product is priced at less than $100, you should spend less of your advertising budget on creating sales literature. If your product is priced at more than $300, you should spend more. A person interested in buying a new car will be better sold by a beautifully designed four-color brochure than by a one-page black-and-white data sheet. The logic behind this is that if your product's purchase price is high, you'll want to spend more on these kinds of promotions. In sales literature, image, a consistent image, *is* everything.

■ Sales Literature Checklist

✓ In general, your sales literature plan should be guided by the price and quality of your product. Do you have an overall plan for your sales literature? Does your literature have a consistent look and feel?

✓ Have you written data sheets for customers and/or distributors?

✓ Have you designed an effective brochure?

✓ Do you have a rate card?

✓ Have you written the form letters you will need?

✓ Do you have a realistic budget for your sales literature?

■ Review Questions

1. What is sales literature and why is it necessary?

2. What information should be included in a data sheet?

3. It is a good idea to come up with a "portfolio" of brochures. Which different brochures are necessary?

4. What is a rate card and why is it useful?

5. Why should you create form letters?

6. How should you decide to allocate your sales literature budget?

■ Activities

1. Write your data sheet for one product for your target customer. Use the Sales Support Collateral Materials section of the Marketing Communications template (2-MARCOM.DOC) to assist you.

2. Sketch out the design of your brochure, including content, layout, and necessary elements. Use the Corporate Capabilities Brochure and Sales Support Collateral Materials section of the Marketing Communications template (2-MARCOM.DOC).

3. Sketch out a rate card. Use the Sales Support Collateral Materials section of the Marketing Communications template (2-MARCOM.DOC) to assist you.

4. Create the following form letters: (a) response to customer inquiry letter, (b) customer thank-you note, and (c) response to customer complaint letter.

Chapter 12

Advertising

Advertising is the creation and placement of messages to selected audiences to inform potential customers and solicit sales of your products and services. Advertisements are any paid communication vehicles for the benefit of their sponsors.

Advertisements can be displayed in many different ways: on television, in publications, on the radio, on outdoor billboards, through direct mail, on mass transit vehicles, in the Yellow Pages, online, and on point-of-purchase displays in stores. The medium you choose will depend on your creativity, your budget, your target market, your message, and the cost.

Advertising is a more long-term approach to increasing sales than sales promotions or personal selling. One advertisement can reach millions of people at one time. Or, it can be a personal one-to-one medium of targeted direct mail. Either method you choose will depend on a variety of factors.

Advertising works best when your target market strategy is to solicit business from a large potential market. This is because the cost per person reached can be very low. Advertising, however, can also be very effective in more narrowly defined markets, if you find the right vehicle to reach them. With local newspapers, radio, and television, you can effectively reach a geographically defined market segment.

 **Learning Objectives**

After completing this chapter, you should be able to:

1. Know what creative aspects can enhance advertising
2. Understand media alternatives, choose a media mix, and design a media plan
3. Target direct mail and manage lists
4. Manage product promotion aspects such as brand names, logos, and packaging
5. Set an advertising budget
6. Consider using advertising agencies
7. Test communications efforts

■ Be Creative

Creativity is so very important in letting your message get its point across to your target audience. If you do only what other companies have done or stick to a familiar creative format, there's a good chance your ad will not have the desired impact and return on its investment.

Arouse Emotions

One way to get your message across to consumers is to strike a familiar emotional chord in them. If people are touched on an emotional or personal level by your ad, they are much more likely to remember that ad consciously.

Stick in Their Minds

Jingles or slogans can be an effective way to catch consumers' attention and stick your company's name in their minds. Anything that repeats itself will eventually stick in people's minds. In advertising, that is called frequency.

Be Funny

Humor can be an extremely effective tool to catch people's attention. Humor for humor's sake, though, is unlikely to work. But humor as part of the whole message can bring originality to your ad campaign.

Use a Presenter

Many companies choose to use a presenter in their advertisements. Presenters or spokespeople can include famous celebrities, special characters created for the ad campaign, a lifestyle representative, or an anonymous individual. Again, you must think about what you're trying to achieve and what you can spend.

Some characteristics you might look for in a presenter are visibility (popularity), credibility, attractiveness, and power.

What Motivates Them?

What kind of motivation will get your target market to buy your product? There are two general kinds of motivation: positive and negative. You must decide what will motivate potential customers to buy your product and use that information.

Positive motivation sends the message that good things will happen if a consumer uses your product. Negative motivation communicates that something bad will happen if consumers don't buy your product.

■ Design Your Media Plan

Your media plan should be designed to expose your product to the largest possible segment of your target market in the most effective, efficient way. The two main components of your media plan will be media selection and media scheduling (or buying).

Media Selection

Media selection answers the question *Where?* You need to find out the best places to advertise so that the greatest number of target customers see your ads. You can get media kits from the different media, such as magazines, newspapers, or television and radio stations, to determine which vehicle best reaches customers of your products. A reader, viewer, or listener profile that the media provides will help you decide what the best vehicle is for your market.

Using advertising or media agencies for this purpose often makes sense because they know what is out there and they have experience at negotiating price. Agencies are often paid a percentage (or commission) of what you normally pay to the media. In other words, they get a discount from the media outlet, so that they can take that commission as a fee for services rendered. The standard media commission is 15 percent.

Media Scheduling

Media scheduling answers the questions *When?* and *How often?* Depending on your objectives and your target market, you'll have widely differing answers to these questions.

The *when* will change if you're about to launch a new product, you want to time your ad campaign with the beginning of some event or you want the campaign to work in conjunction with sales promotions.

How often you repeat the ad will depend on how long you believe it will take to get the message across to the consumer and how big your advertising media budget is.

■ Test Your Communications Efforts

Test your promotions before you complete the final production and media schedule. Even if you have spent a certain amount of money to come up with and design the campaign, you need to make sure it will do the job. There's always a risk in using new and creative ideas—not all will work. Just remember, if you refuse to pull the plug on a bad ad campaign, you'll lose more than money. You'll lose customers, too.

■ Target Your Direct Mail

Direct mail can be a very effective way to advertise your product. Direct mail is flexible, which means that you can tailor it to fit your needs.

Techniques

To make your direct mail effective, you need to think creatively to entice your target audience to read what you send them. The first thing people will see is your envelope, so you should try to think of a way to make it stand out. Once the reader has opened the envelope, you can pull him or her in further with an effective headline. The same holds true for postcard mailers. Your headline must offer the reader something, a promise or benefit. You may want to offer free shipping or other incentives to buy, along with a clever headline.

Your order form should be a call to action. Put your price and terms on the order form, not in the main body of the mailer. You can also give your readers the option to request more information. You might also leave space for people to list other folks they think might be interested in your product. The use of an 800 number is a surefire easy way for your customers to order. That 800 number should be easy to spot on the mailer and on the order form itself. The rule of thumb: "Make it as easy to buy as possible."

Budgeting Your Direct Mail Campaign

Direct mail is effective in generating end-user demand and easily tracked results. You can use many different types of direct mail, ranging from product upgrades, information updates, new product announcements, contests, to a sales announcement.

You need to decide how direct mail can benefit your business and set measurable goals. Calculate the cost to send direct mail to the number of potential customers on your mailing list. Then, figure the return you expect as a percent as a result of that campaign. You can then easily calculate how much money that direct mail campaign will generate. What level of profit would you have at each response rate? By doing this, you can gauge how likely you are to earn a profit, and can decide whether it's worthwhile to make this investment.

Before starting your direct mail activities, go to your local post office and request a copy of *The Mailer's Guide*. It contains abridged information on bulk mailing permits, mail classification items, customer service programs, and other useful information. Then, make sure that you find the most economical way to do your mass mailings. You can hire a direct mail company to put together a mail campaign for you—it may be wise to contact one.

■ Manage Your Lists

List management can target your market via databases of names and addresses of your current and potential customers. To successfully carry out a direct mail campaign, you need to have your own customer lists or rent potential customer lists from a list brokerage company.

Mailing lists can be purchased for your target markets, but the best, most effective lists are developed in-house. Your existing customer file is the most likely set of buyers for your new products. Registration cards and/or periodic surveys will build your customer list and measure the success of your marketing activities by providing a historical profile of your customer.

In addition to your current and potential customer mailing lists, you'll also want to keep a current list of press contacts and industry analysts. This list is really part of your public relations efforts. If an outside agency does your PR, they would most likely maintain and update this list. To systematically build your list, have everyone who comes in contact with customers, prospects, the press, and others capture names, addresses, and other pertinent information in a contact management system. Whether it's computerized or manual, the accumulation of these names has value for your company's effective marketing with direct mail.

■ Explore Internet Opportunities

As interactive computer and television technology advances, possibilities are evolving for two-way advertising on interactive kiosks, home shopping networks, and online computer networks such as the Internet's interactive branch, the World Wide Web. The World Wide Web is becoming an increasingly popular vehicle for advertisers.

■ Package to Sell

The way your package is designed, its shape, size, color, and material, can be crucial to your success in selling your product to the general public or to another business. The package or box is a very important way to get attention and arouse interest in your product. Your packaging can be a silent, yet highly persuasive, product promoter. If several comparable products are on the market, the consumer may choose a product by the package. This is especially true with low-risk products, products that don't require a large investment, such as food items.

To create a successful design for your packaging, take into account what you found out about your target market. What your packaging looks like on the outside is important, but what you put inside the package is also very important. Keep all information as simple and clear as possible and direct it to your target audience. There are many firms that do nothing but design and build packaging. You can hire them or perhaps hire a freelance graphic designer to design your box. Whatever you do, spend the time to plan the right package that sells both on the store shelf and in your sales literature and advertising.

■ Create Your Brand Name and Logo

Establishing strong brand name recognition can be a great asset in marketing your product. To create a brand name, an important rule is to keep it simple. If you choose a clever company or product name that different people pronounce different ways, you may have trouble getting customers over the long run.

You should also make sure to choose a name that will be timeless. Avoid using gimmicky names that are likely to lose significance over time. If your product is associated with a fad because of its name, your sales will probably drop as the fad passes. Try to come up with a name that is easy to recognize and remember. If someone reads about your product or sees an advertisement for it but can't remember the name when it comes time to buy, you'll lose a sale.

Additionally, a logo should be simple, easy to recognize, and memorable.

If a customer sees a familiar name or logo and associates quality with that name, your chances of selling to that customer greatly improve. If five similar products are on display, the customer is most likely to choose what is familiar.

Some companies specialize in developing product names and logo design. You may better serve yourself and your company by hiring an outside design firm to do your logo, while you dedicate your efforts to what you know how to do best.

■ Your Advertising Budget

Your advertising budget defines and sets limits as to how much money you plan to spend on advertising during a given period. Advertising can be quite expensive, so make sure you're getting a good return on your investment. Is a certain advertising vehicle paying for itself, either with trackable sales or increased awareness? When you first launch your company or a new product, advertising may not pay dividends immediately. But by keeping good records, you'll eventually start to see the effort pay off.

■ The Media

In this section, we will go into a little more depth about the different types of media available for advertising your company and its products and services.

Network Television

A commercial on network TV can reach more potential customers with one message than any other form of advertising. The major networks are ABC, NBC, CBS, and FOX. Two new networks have started, UPN and Warner Bros. When you buy commercials on a network, you buy time in one of its programs. Network television time can cost hundreds of thousands of dollars for one 30-second spot during a popular program. You may need to find other ways to reach your customers.

Local Television

Local TV (sometimes called Spot TV) is much like network television; but it is confined to a local geographic area and the cost for spots is much less. Call a local TV station and have their sales rep show you which of their shows can deliver the highest number of viewers that fit your customer profile for the least amount of dollars. In most markets, you can buy UHF (channels 2 to 13) or VHF (14 to 60). (UHF channels traditionally are the network affiliates, while VHF channels are the independents.)

Cable TV

Cable television is becoming a more important medium all the time. Cable viewership is smaller than the more traditional form of television, but cable TV has a loyal, upscale, growing audience. You buy spots in programming just as you do on local or network TV.

One important feature of cable TV is its cost. Many spots are very inexpensive and are priced more along the lines of radio time. So, here, a few dollars can go a long way. Although the total size of the audience may be smaller when compared to network TV, it is still a good advertising vehicle.

Local Radio

Local radio is an excellent medium for local businesses. When you buy radio spots, you are buying time sold in either 60-second, 30-second, or 10-second "IDs." The length of spots you should buy depends on the content of your message, your creative approach, and the amount of time you need.

To best utilize local radio and increase your advertising frequency, you must advertise for a multiple of weeks, not just one. Most people listen to radio in specific time periods. (Think what time you listen to the radio—it's usually the same time each day.) So, to reach more potential customers, you need to run more spots over a longer period of time than just one week.

When purchasing radio time, you must consider the type of programming format that each station has. Obviously, one station doesn't appeal to every listener. Each station's format appeals to a demographic group of listeners.

To determine how many people are listening to any particular station at any given time period, you can study rating books. An Arbitron rating book lists the number of people of a certain age group (say, 25- to 54-year-old men) in any given quarter hour.

One more thing to think about is the cumulative figure which is the number of different people who listen at one time. Your local radio station sales rep will be more than happy to show you the ratings but beware—they can be confusing to even the most experienced radio time buyer. When dealing with any media representative, it is often the best policy to go with your "gut" feeling to choose a station that will do the best job for your business.

Network Radio

Like network television, if your business is national or regional, you can purchase time on a radio network. Some of the well-known radio networks are NBC, CBS, ABC, and Mutual. You can run a flight of spots or purchase specific programming, such as an hourly news broadcast or the major league baseball game of the week. Also, the syndicated programs of Don Imus, Howard Stern, or Rush Limbaugh are simulcast over dozens of stations nationwide where you can advertise.

Outdoor Advertising

Outdoor advertising, which includes billboards, transit ads (taxi and bus signs), and even signage on park benches and inside buses and airports, is a great medium to deliver a simple message to a large audience fast. Outdoor ads are sold in "showings," which refers to the number of billboards or "posters" you can buy.

The typical billboard is called a "poster" or "30 sheet" and is the most common. It is the sign you see most often along highways and is made of printed paper that is hung on the sign front. The next classification is painted bulletins (sometimes on walls), and the last is the "spectacular," which can be any size (or shape) and is usually electric.

Outdoor ads are a great medium if you want to introduce a new product that appeals to a wide audience, such as a new brand of breakfast cereal or a new restaurant location. You measure outdoor advertising's worth by the gross circulation, or the number of people who pass its location in a single day. You rent the board on a monthly basis, and each message you have can be "rotated" to a different location each month to spread the advertising message around to different audiences.

Newspapers

Advertising in the local newspaper is a fast and efficient way to reach your target audience. The advantage of newspaper ads is that readers usually pay to read them. When you purchase space in a newspaper, you buy it by the column inch. Most newspapers have frequency discounts when you run a number of ads, so the cost per column inch will go down. Check the rate cards to see what other discounts you might earn.

We may be used to the daily paper being delivered to your front door each day, but many smaller communities have weeklies or biweekly papers. These are still good advertising mediums for local advertisers. The reproduction of ads is not very good in these papers when compared to magazines, so keep that in mind when designing ads and using colors. Black-and-white is still the ad of choice, even in the '90s.

One drawback of newspapers is the lack of longevity. Your ad is seen on only one day and then is gone. So, the newspaper is a good reach medium but a poor one for frequency.

The U.S. doesn't have many national newspapers. Most notable are the *Wall Street Journal* and *USA Today*. If you want to reach a national audience, you should also consider magazines.

Free Standing Insert

Free Standing Inserts (FSI) are coupons and flyers that come in your paper. These are preprinted by advertisers and are distributed by the newspapers based on a cost per thousand (CPM). FSIs can be in high-quality four-color printing because they are printed by the advertiser and not the newspaper. Such high-quality printing is perfect for advertising food items.

Magazines

Depending on your product, and your target demographic audience, the use of magazines is perhaps one of the best and most effective mediums in advertising. In the U.S. alone, thousands of different magazines cover every type of business activity, every leisure pastime, every political persuasion imaginable. Surely you can think of at least one magazine that has editorial coverage of your business, perhaps two or three more.

The advertising reference guide *Standard Rate and Data,* or *SRDS ,* lists all these magazines. There is an *SRDS* for every medium, including TV, radio, newspapers, outdoor, direct mail, and so on. To verify a magazine's circulation, ask for its ABC reports (Audit Bureau of Circulation) for paid circulation publications and BPA (Business Press Audit) reports for nonpaid ones.

With magazines, you can target just the group of customers you need to reach. Because every industry or special interest group has its own periodical, the opportunity to target your potential customers is almost as good as the use of direct mail.

The size of your ad in magazines is determined by your creative needs for space and by the size of your budget. You can purchase space in a magazine in multipage inserts, spreads, single full pages, 2/3, 1/2, 1/3, or 1/4 page units in black-and-white, two, three, and four colors. Your creative design will dictate what size to use and if you need to use four colors or not. You can save money by using black-and-white with a second color, for example, and still get impact among all the four-color ads.

Direct Mail

Billions of dollars are spent on direct mail every year in this country, and for good reason. It is the most trackable medium you can use to advertise your products or services. If you follow a few rules of thumb in executing direct mail campaigns, you'll have a better chance of success with your next mailing.

The List

The most important element of successful direct mail is the mailing list. Without a good list of prospective customers, no matter how good the offer or how creative the mailer itself is, the mailing will fail to generate the sales you want.

The best mailing list is your own current customer list. These people have already bought from you and know your company and your products. Mail to these people first. If you have done your market analysis, you will have a demographic outline of your average customer. You can then go to a direct marketing firm or a list broker and rent other mailing lists with a target profile match to your current customers. This rented list should produce good results for you, because those people are like your existing customers.

Mailing lists are rented by the thousands, with most minimum orders being 5,000 names. Be sure to check the quality of the list you rent, because outdated or poorly maintained lists will be a prescription for failure.

The Offer

The offer is the next important element in a successful mailing. You might want to consider a special price, two-for-one, buy-one-get-one-free, or purchase-today-for-free-air-express-delivery offer, and so on. Direct mail is designed to make it easy for your customers to order today. By having a solid promotional offer, you increase the likelihood of success.

To make it easy to order, include a toll-free 800 number, a prepaid business reply card (BRC) or envelope (BRE), a fax number for ordering, and an e-mail or Internet address. Accept all major credit cards (VISA, MasterCard, American Express, Discover) and personal and business checks. However the customer wants to buy, make the option available and you will see a remarkable increase in your orders.

The Creativity

The last element is the creative content of your mailing piece. If the U.S. Post Office will accept it, then any type of mailing piece is worth a try. Whether you mail a simple postcard, a business letter, a packet with letter, a brochure, a BRC, or a full catalog in its own envelope, the idea is that the recipient opens and reads your offer. Getting the mailer open and read is its first job.

You might want to consider printing a "teaser" line on the outside of the mailer to entice the customer to open the envelope. Or, use the word "free" on the outside, such as, "Get a free software upgrade when you purchase any two programs." Once the mailer is opened, the offer should be clear and easy to understand. Include a brochure or other information about the product or service, add customer success stories and editorial reviews, and be sure to have that "way to order" mechanism bold and easy to find and read.

One of the downsides to direct mail is its image as "junk" mail. In direct mail, good response rate is 1 percent to 3 percent of the pieces mailed. Many direct mail companies can assist you in design, printing, list rental, and lettershop (or mailing).

Yellow Pages

Consumers who use the Yellow Pages to look up products have already made a buying decision and now are looking to find the right business at the right location. If your business is a retail or service, Yellow Pages is a must for you. The local telephone company Yellow Pages' sales rep can provide rates and help you with the design and layout of your ad.

Remember that an ad in the Yellow Pages lasts for one year, so make sure you have covered all the important points about your business in your ad, such as name and logo, address, type of service or product, and perhaps a little "sell" copy about your business. If your location is important, be sure to add a map. Remember to have your telephone number nice and big in your ad!

Finally, you may wish to have Yellow Pages ads in more than one directory, not just the one in your area. If your store is the only one of its type in the city, it is worthwhile to advertise in other directories to reach customers who are miles from you. Many large national advertisers such as airlines put ads in all directories to make it convenient for their customers to find their telephone number. Again, make it as easy as possible for your customers to find and buy from you.

Telemarketing

The telephone is a very powerful tool in marketing. Used in the right way, it can be a valuable addition to your marketing mix. Telemarketing consists of both outbound and inbound telephone calls. A company that uses direct mail should have a well-organized telemarketing system in place to handle customer orders by phone. A computerized system allows your operators to enter orders on screen and to follow a sales script when speaking with customers.

Outbound telemarketing can be effective if used in conjunction with other marketing promotions. Say that you mail a promotional piece offering a business update service. Your prospective customer receives the mailer but has yet to act on it. If you follow up with a phone call to them, the combination of direct mail and telemarketing can increase order rates dramatically.

There is a big drawback, however, with outbound telemarketing. Many people are annoyed when they receive a sales phone call. The federal and state governments have even stepped in with new laws regarding telemarketing, such as what hours you can call a person's home and how the caller is identified. So, be very sure that your sales calls are done legally and won't turn off potential customers before you launch an outbound telemarketing program.

■ Consider Your Media Mix

When choosing where to advertise, you should request media kits from the various publications or stations where you might want to advertise. A media kit is an information packet that provides the demographics of the media's subscribers, circulation, readership, listeners, or viewership as well as their rate cards. These demographics should identify what type of customer reads the newspaper or magazine, listens to that radio station, or watches a television channel. In addition, media kits often include information on consumers' buying habits and other demographic and psychographic data. Your job is to match your target market with the demographics of a particular media in order to select the best advertising vehicle for your business. The chart on the next two pages summarizes the advantages and disadvantages of various advertising media.

■ The Advertising Agency

The one advantage of hiring an ad agency is that they specialize in advertising; they bring experience and expertise to what they produce. Ad agencies bring an outside perspective and fresh ideas to company. It's this outside perspective that can be very important if your company wishes to bring a new look and direction to your advertising.

On the downside, ad agencies can be expensive, and you may lose some of *your* vision to *their* vision. Because of their expertise, however, an ad agency might save you a great deal of time and money. Remember, the ad agency works for you as a partner to develop and implement successful advertising campaigns.

The advertising agency is made up of different departments. These are account services, media, creative, and, in some agencies, research or planning. Your contact with all departments in the agency should be coordinated by the account group, usually by an Account Executive (AE).

Advertising agencies are often paid a commission, from the media discounts they earn, from production markups, and increasingly from fees. The standard commission charged by an advertising agency is 15 percent.

Some ad agencies charge various fees for their services. Sometimes, it's an hourly rate or just a flat fee. Be sure to ask up front how the ad agency makes its money before you hire them. To find out which ad agency may be right for your company, ask other businesses for recommendations or contact the American Association of Advertising Agencies, known as the four As. Be sure to evaluate your agency's performance after you hire them.

Market Brief

 Advantages and Disadvantages of Advertising Media

Medium	Advantages	Disadvantages
Network television	Most powerful image/awareness advertising vehicle Both visual and audio capabilities Mass market reach Good sponsorship/control opportunities Can sponsor sports and other programming Very high HH ratings and low CPM	Very high cost per spot Difficult to buy specific target markets Very competitive market All time can be sold out Need top-quality commercial production values, very expensive to produce spots Only four major networks
Outdoor and transit	Very high repeat exposure Very low CPM Large, colorful medium Can target different geographic areas, neighborhoods, and highways Length of time to show message: 30 days Better to keep same ad and move billboard than to keep same billboard and change ad	High total cost for large showings High cost of 'painted spectacular' billboard locations Highway 'clutter' problem Limited format options for creative message Difficult to reach specific target market
Cable TV	Powerful image/awareness generator Medium CPM Local target market programming Inexpensive production costs High frequency potential Dozens of different cable networks to choose from	Limited reach in some markets due to low cable penetration Very low HH Deficient coverage in some markets Cable monopoly in all markets
Network and local radio	Cost effective with very high frequency, low CPM Target selection by programming and by station formats Good support medium Excellent audio capability and stereo on FM dial Reaches broad market Reaches captive audience, i.e., commuters Excellent creative medium by creating mental images	No visual capability Considered background noise by some listeners Must purchase lots of different stations and spots to reach large market Poor reception in many markets

Source: *Business Age Magazine*, Vol. 2, No. 8, August 1988.

Market Brief

Newspapers	High local market penetration	Weak or limited color
	Some targeting by section	Size equals degree of impact
	Direct response capabilities	Higher cost for special positioning
	Current or immediate message and announcement	Limited reproduction quality
	Short lead time to place ad	Short exposure (only one day)
	Medium-high to low CPM	Lots of clutter
Free-standing insert	Low cost, low CPM	Clutter problem
	Good for coupons and mail order	Low target capability
	Good local market coverage	Discount image
	Good for catalog-type advertising	Potential junk mail image
	Good color reproduction	Long lead time for insertions
Magazines	Moderate to excellent targeting	High CPM
	Great image medium	Long lead time (60 to 90 days)
	Good direct-response capability	Incomplete control over ad location
	Longer message shelf life	
	Multiple readers per issue	
	High-quality reproduction	
	Weekly or monthly frequency	
	Thousands to choose from and many targeted to specific industries	
Direct Mail	Best medium for targeting prospects	High CPM
	Good awareness and sales conversion	High up-front testing and list acquisition costs
	Unlimited format options for message and layout	Low response rates
	Private medium	High postal rates
	Easy to personalize	Slow delivery times
Yellow Pages	Low CPM	Limited to active shoppers only
	Consumers are already buyers for your products	Ad often right next to competitors'
	High potential exposure	Limited creative options
	Very localized	Ad lasts one year, can't change
Telemarketing	Effective in conjunction with existing advertising	Very high CPM
	Instant customer feedback	High cost of telephone lists
	Highly personal	Format limitations
	Easy to implement and timely	Poor image and very intrusive
		Low close rates

■ Advertising Checklist

✓ How creative are your ads? Will they stick in the customer's mind? Have you considered using humor? If you're using a presenter, is that person effective?

✓ Have you selected the most effective places to advertise? Where are you going to advertise?

✓ Have you scheduled your media effectively? When and how often will you advertise?

✓ Have you tested your advertising?

✓ Are you using direct mail effectively? Do you have a good mailing list?

✓ Have you considered advertising on the Internet?

✓ Does your product have a successful package?

✓ Have you maximized brand recognition through a strong brand name and logo?

✓ Do you have a realistic budget for advertising?

✓ Have you requested media kits from all the publications or stations you are considering?

✓ Have you picked an ad agency that meets your needs?

■ Review Questions

1. What creative methods can be used in advertising to get the advertising message across to audiences?

2. List all the possible media that could be used for an advertising campaign.

3. What are the elements of a media plan?

4. How can lists of customers be obtained and managed?

5. What are some elements of a successful brand name? Why is it good to associate a logo with the brand name?

■ Activities

1. List some objectives of your advertising campaign. Use the Promotion and Advertising Campaign portions of the Marketing Communications template (2-MARCOM.DOC) to assist you.

2. List all the media options available to your firm. Choose a mix of these media that should be most effective for your product. Then design an advertising/media schedule. Use the Preliminary Media Schedule portion of the Marketing Communications template (2-MARCOM.DOC) and the Advertising Schedule template (AD-SCHED.DOC) to assist you.

3. Design an advertisement using one of the media selected above, keeping in mind creativity aspects described in this chapter. Remember to use your brand name and logo (design these if necessary).

4. Describe a possible direct mail campaign for your firm.

5. Estimate your advertising campaign budget.

6. Evaluate past advertising campaigns or set up an evaluation plan for current or future campaigns.

Chapter 13

Public Relations

 **Learning Objectives**

While advertising is "what you say about yourself," public relations is "what you get others to say about you." Public relations (also called PR) is information about your company, your product, your project, or your event that isn't a direct message from you to the potential customer.

After completing this chapter, you should be able to:

1. Set public relations objectives

2. Select public relations strategies and activities

3. Devise the public relations budget

4. Evaluate public relations agencies

Public relations efforts result in publicity. Publicity is usually reported by an independent party, such as a newspaper, trade magazine, or television or radio news program. You don't pay directly for publicity, but its value to you in sales can be dramatic.

Consumers very often assume that third-party, objective reports about companies and products are more reliable. Potential customers are often more likely to react to what they believe is an unbiased opinion or suggestion than to advertisements. Often, the consumers that are least likely to react to advertisements and promotions are the most likely to react to PR.

■ Establish PR Objectives

Just as with every other aspect of your marketing plan, you should know what you're trying to achieve through your public relations activities. A primary consideration of the PR for a company must be directed at what audience (or audiences) you are trying to influence and what message (or messages) they need to hear. You need to consider whether you can handle your public relations in-house or whether you want to hire a firm that dedicates itself to PR in your industry.

■ Devise PR Strategies

Once you've decided to include public relations, *thinking through* your program is the first and most important step you take. In developing PR strategies, think about how you can realistically meet your objectives with the resources at hand. For a given objective, probably several different strategies can be taken. Consider addressing some of the following areas in your PR activities.

Publications

Try to inform industry or general interest publications about what your company is doing, especially if you're doing something new and different. Magazines and trade journals often reach a narrow market of readers interested in your industry. Enthusiasts with specific interests look to these publications to inform them of the latest products and trends.

Introducing your product to people who work at industry publications is also a good way to gauge the public response you're likely to get. If the editor of an industry journal is completely baffled by your product, that might be the response you get from the market in general. On the other hand, if that editor is enthusiastic about what you have to offer and asks to be kept up-to-date on your product release, you'll have a good idea that you're headed in the right direction.

News Publications

If you're doing something that is newsworthy, make sure the general press knows about it. Consider how your company and its projects might interest news organizations. Most newspapers have columns that cover a wide range of activities and topics.

Events

Sponsoring events is one way to gain exposure for your company and potentially win over a whole set of consumers. If you choose this method, be sure to pick events that interest your target market. You need to weigh the cost of undertaking such an activity against the benefits it will bring to your company.

Speeches

Speeches provide another way to gain recognition. Try to set your company or its executives up as experts in your field. If consumers see that the CEO, president, or other employee of your company is articulate, intelligent, and well informed, they are likely to have more trust in your company and its products. If consumers see that the media or government looks to your company to provide expertise, that will likely provide you with even more credibility. Before you send someone out to make speeches, be certain that they will make a good impression. You should consider small events, such as graduations, that are covered by local newspapers. Professional coaching in giving speeches can be a cost-effective way to insure better responses to speeches presented.

Public Service Activities

Involvement in public service activities is another way to gain exposure for your company and a favorable profile in your community. This type of action promotes goodwill and could be the deciding factor when a consumer chooses between your product and a competitor's.

■ Plan Your PR Budget

Allocating money for public relations is especially important in the product introductory phase. In that phase, you want to let as many people as possible know about your product. To come up with a PR budget, you'll have to decide which PR tools you want to use and what the expected return on each is likely to be. PR can be a relatively inexpensive way to gain wide exposure, but it must be well planned and properly executed. Your PR budget should allocate enough funds to keep the press up-to-date on company developments; that is, someone in your company needs enough time to develop and distribute good, newsworthy press releases.

■ Write Press Releases

Press releases are prepared statements that can be distributed to various media outlets. You can prepare a press release for any important development in your company: a new product or product line, service area, product upgrade, technical development, participation in a major event, and awards for your product, personnel, service, or performance.

A press release should, obviously, contain only information you want to become public, that sheds a positive light on your company or product. Include a black-and-white glossy photo of your product or an interesting demo of your product, if possible.

■ Invite Editors to Visit

Inviting the most influential reporters and editors from targeted publications and media outlets for a visit is important to maintain high visibility in the marketplace. During the visit, each of the editors and reporters should receive a complete tour of your facility. The tour should include a product briefing and an opportunity to interview the chairperson, the president, and the product and marketing managers.

■ Create a Corporate Newsletter

An internal or external newsletter serves as an informational piece for office personnel, the sales force, and key customers. An internal newsletter serves the purpose of keeping employees in touch with the company's overall operations and successes and better able to serve your customers.

The point of sending an external newsletter to customers, potential customers, and the press is to create and foster a positive image of your company. You should include profiles of satisfied customers, community projects, information on forthcoming products, a message from the CEO, and timely information related to your product or industry.

The PR Agency

You have much to consider when you choose to hire a public relations agency. An agency has experience and can bring expertise to your PR efforts. Ask other businesses for referrals. See if any firms specialize in your industry.

Also, consider whether you want to hire a large PR firm or a small one. There is no right answer in deciding which size firm to choose. You must decide what services you want an agency to provide you and find one that can do those to your satisfaction.

Compensation

Public relations professionals generally charge for their expertise in blocks of time. The charges may be by the hour, the day, the project, or through monthly or annual retainer. You can also be billed for out-of-pocket expenses incurred on your behalf, such as travel, lodging, entertainment, postage, and so on. When negotiating an agreement-for-hire fee with your PR firm, remember:

- PR professionals and agencies are in business to make money
- Clients must provide a budget that allows adequate time to meet their goals

Understand also that allocating twice as much budget results in twice as much effort and time, but not necessarily twice the results. Results are a function of many components, including but not limited to your message, positioning, and money spent on PR. As a client, you should stay aware of the time a PR firm allots to your account. This will prevent surprises on your bill, because, in PR, time is money.

Public Relations Checklist

✓ Have you set objectives for your PR campaign?

✓ Have you spent time thinking through your PR strategy? Have you considered which avenues you're going to use, such as industry and/or general interest publications, news publications, event sponsorship, and public service activities?

✓ Have you planned your PR budget?

✓ Do you have written press releases?

✓ Have you considered publishing a corporate newsletter?

✓ Have you selected a PR agency that meets your needs?

■ Review Questions

1. What is the primary advantage of getting publicity through your public relations activities?

2. List the possible public relations tools you could use to achieve publicity.

3. When during the product life cycle is PR most important?

4. Everyone hears about "free publicity." Are public relations and the resultant publicity free?

■ Activities

1. Set public relations goals and objectives. Use the Public Relations portion of the Marketing Communications template (2-MARCOM.DOC) to assist you.

2. Set your public relations budget.

3. Write a press release about your featured product or service.

4. Design an internal or external corporate newsletter (at least the first sample page). Include this information in the Public Relations portion of the Marketing Communications template (2-MARCOM.DOC).

Chapter 14

Trade Shows

Major shows command year-round attention, with preparations for the following year's show beginning as soon as this year's show is over! With this level of planning, preparation, and expense, you must be sure your preparation is geared towards maximizing your success.

 **Learning Objectives**

After completing this chapter, you should be able to:

1. Select the appropriate show(s) for your firm

2. Generate media contacts

3. Research the competition

4. Obtain feedback from consumers

5. Generate sales at a trade show

Trade shows offer many advantages if you plan ahead and know what purpose you want to achieve by attending. Trade shows let you connect with key media players, evaluate the competition, talk with consumers, and sell your product. The trick is to choose the best shows for you to attend, and then plan ahead to get the maximum return on your investment.

■ Which Show Is for You?

To help you choose which trade shows to attend, you should request media kits from their organizers. Trade show media kits provide you with a demographic and psychographic profile of who is likely to attend the show. This way, you can calculate approximately how many people are likely to come to your booth and what their wants and needs are.

■ Meeting the Media Players

Use trade shows as a way to maintain a high profile with editors of key media. Editors and reporters from a variety of newspapers, magazines, and television and radio stations attend trade shows. You can impress a wide range of journalists by having a professional booth with well thought-out sales literature and demos.

Take the opportunity to schedule any major product announcements to coincide with a trade show, because you'll have greater access to the media. If you do have a product or other major announcement, plan it well in advance so that you'll get the maximum number of people to attend the show and have the greatest possible impact. Good relationships with the media are an asset, and trade shows provide the opportunity to establish and foster those relationships.

■ Checking Out the Competitors

Trade shows are an excellent time to evaluate the competition and expand your knowledge of other products in your industry. With many of your competitors gathered in one place, at one time, all giving their best sales pitches and literature out for free, research can't get any easier. Knowing what the competition is doing is key in developing your marketing strategies.

■ Learning from Consumers

Trade shows also allow you to meet potential customers and talk with them. Many companies have small giveaways that people get if they fill out a short survey or provide their business cards. This is a convenient way to find out more about your customers and can be a valuable part of your market research.

Remember to follow up on the information you receive. If you conduct a short survey (possibly in the form of a prize drawing), include questions that will help you better understand your customers' wants and needs. Then, don't forget to read and analyze what you find. If you collect business cards, identify individuals from companies that are likely to buy your product and do short phone interviews with them or send them direct mail. You can also add these names to your mailing list and target direct mail and promotions to those people.

■ Generating Sales

Trade shows also give you the opportunity to sell your product. People go to trade shows because they want to find out what is available. Many companies advertise trade show specials that offer discounts for sales or orders at the show.

While trade shows can be a very cost-effective way to reach your target market, you must *follow through* on your prospects to make the experience worthwhile. There's great potential value in pitching your product at a show and being highly visible to consumers and the media, but it does take some effort. You don't want to waste your time and money, so plan ahead and follow up afterwards.

■ Trade Shows Checklist

✓ Have you requested media kits from the shows you're interested in attending?

✓ Have you planned your trade show booth, activities, and so on? See the Trade Show Checklist and Schedule in Part 4.

✓ Have you timed key announcements to coincide with trade shows?

✓ Do you have a plan for checking out your competitors at the trade show?

✓ Have you thought about how you're going to follow through with consumers who stop by your booth?

■ Review Questions

1. How can you best choose the right trade show(s) for you?

2. Who should you be visiting with at trade shows?

3. How can you generate sales by attending a trade show?

■ Activities

1. Search for possible trade shows that are appropriate for your company to attend. (If accessible to you, the *Eventline* database and other online services allow searches of trade shows). Use the Trade Show Checklist and Schedule template (TRADECHK.DOC) to complete this task and evaluate the options.

2. Cover trade show information in the Trade Show portion of the Marketing Communications template (2-MARCOM.DOC).

Chapter 15

Customer Service

Customer service is a key component to attracting and retaining customers. Your marketing communications, advertising, and PR efforts don't end with getting people to buy; you also want to retain their loyalty. Customer service, while a form of promotion in itself, can lead to perhaps the most powerful form of promotion, that is, word-of-mouth recommendations by customers who are thrilled to do business with you.

 **Learning Objectives**

After completing this chapter, you should be able to:

1. Understand the components of a customer service program, including product instructions and customer communication support

2. Standardize a customer service policy

3. Know how to evaluate customer service operations

■ Developing Your Customer Service Operations

Customer service is important for every type of business. Think about the products your customers are buying and what kind of support they might expect after they bought. You also need to spell out policies regarding product returns, repairs, and dissatisfied customers. It's good to remember that you're not doing your customers a favor by selling them your product; they are doing you the favor by buying it.

Take a clear look at the implications of each of your customer service policies. Can you really afford to staff a phone 24 hours a day, seven days a week? Providing a full refund with no questions asked may attract a wide range of customers, but is there a chance you could lose money by offering this policy? Think each policy through, and do only what you can do well.

■ Creating Clear Product Instructions

In designing your product's operating instructions, make sure that they are clear and easy to understand—written for your customers, not your engineers. This will reduce both buyer remorse and the number of tech support calls you get requesting help and explanations. Always test your instructions on a variety of customers and find out where the instructions can be made clearer. (If you are exporting, consider bilingual or trilingual instructions.)

■ Handling Customer Complaints

It's important to please your customers when they call with a complaint. These complaints should be handled in a timely manner. Remember, there will always be customers who find fault with your product. It's important to listen intently to the customer—ask questions, take notes, make them feel that you are "hearing them out." Then, find reasonable solutions for the customer to choose from. Even if you don't say exactly what the customer wants to hear, if the solution is the customer's choice, they feel back in control, and are usually appeased. It's difficult to stay angry and frustrated when you've spoken your mind to someone who cares, and the solution provided is one that you chose.

■ Standardizing Your Customer Service Policy

Developing a standardized customer service policy provides clarity and direction for your company and your customer support staff. Whether you're a large or small firm, you should make sure that your customers are treated with respect no matter where or how they buy your product. People like to know what to expect from a company, and your customer service policy should be structured so that your customers receive consistent quality of service from the CEO to the janitor.

■ Evaluating Your Customer Service Operations

It's a good idea to check up on your customer service operations periodically. Customers often don't complain; they just choose to go elsewhere. There are different ways you can audit your customer service, depending on the type of business you have and the product you sell. You could send anonymous employees to pose as customers and evaluate how they are treated, or you could directly ask customers to fill out questionnaires about your customer service. Evaluation is key to most endeavors.

■ Customer Service Checklist

✓ Have you investigated your competition's customer service policies?

✓ Are your product instructions clear?

✓ Have you considered how you can use your customer service as a selling point in your advertising?

✓ Do you have a standardized policy for dealing with dissatisfied customers?

✓ Do you periodically audit your customer service operation?

■ Review Questions

1. List the ways that you can provide customer support.

2. How should customer complaints be handled?

3. Why is it important to standardize your customer service policy?

■ Activities

1. Research the customer service provisions of your key competitors.

2. Review your product instructions to make sure they are clear. Use friends or family members to help test the instructions.

3. Draft a customer service policy to ensure standardization. Use the Customer Service and Returns and Adjustments Policy portions of the Sales Plan template (3-SALES.DOC) to assist you.

4. Evaluate any existing customer service operations.

2-MARCOM.DOC

Marketing Strategy

[*Company's*] _____ marketing strategy is to enhance, promote and support the fact that our products [*list your unique features, benefits, established market position/presence*] _____

_____

_____ .

The overall marketing plan for our product is based on the following fundamentals:

[*Type of business you want to be in*] _____

_____ .

[*Segment of the market(s) you plan to reach*] _____

_____

_____ .

[*Share of the market you expect to capture versus time*] _____

_____

_____ .

When describing how you can prove the value of each product, show each application, demonstrate the effects, and add credibility with scientific reports and studies.

To prove the value of [*product*] _____ we can _____

_____ .

The lack of [*product features/benefits*] _____ in every day [*specific business/professional/manufacturing/shipping/living/household situations*] _____ is demonstrated by _____

_____ .

This information is based on studies of _____

_____ .

Most of the country (and world) are [*describe their situations/circumstances*]

_____

_____

because [*they have problems, continue without your products*] _____

_____ .

Positioning is how customers perceive your company and product, relative to competition (product/business/industry leadership).

A user focus group may provide product information needed to position your product.

Positioning

Our [*product, or similar/competition's product*] _____

is seen by the consumer as [*customer's perception of your product*] _____

_____

_____ .

Its unique advantages [*technical/quality/performance*] _____

_____

can be exploited to arrive at a winning position in the consumer's mind.

In terms of market segmentation advantages, we can use [*upscale consumers/ethnic appeal/etc.*] _____

to arrive at a winning position here.

Repositioning our [*product*] _____ as [*example: from a cost to an investment, vacation becomes an "escape from civilization," etc.*] _____

_____

_____ .

To be effective, [*other products, services, people*] _____

depend on the presence of our [*product*] _____ .

What can be said or shown about a competitor's product that will change your customers' minds (about the competitor's product—not yours)?

We can position against our competitors by _____

_____ .

This is your fundamental strategy for all the advertising you do.

Test the Unique Selling Basis to make sure that it is meaningful, believable, motivating, memorable, simple, logical, and unique.

The resulting Selling Basis for our product, then, is _____

_____

_____

Direct Response Mail

We will be exploring the benefits of incremental, coordinated direct mail programs in the [*example: last two quarters of 19xx*] _____.
We anticipate a strong profit potential as we strengthen our direct response capabilities. We will be approaching this scientifically, as we improve our customer targeting ability. We propose [*example: two 50,000 piece campaigns, each preceded by a 5,000 piece test*] _____
_____.

All direct mail activities this year will be directed to our existing customer base. In addition, we will [*example: test external lists*] _____
_____.

Telemarketing

We will use an [*in-house/contract*] _____ telemarketing service to perform the following functions.

Literature mailing, follow-up calls, order entry, etc.

Provide outside sales support by _____
_____
_____

Order entry, literature mailing, 800# order/support hotline, marketing research, etc.

Respond to inquiries by _____
_____
_____

Contact distributors, retailers, customers; schedule appointments; etc.

Generate new business by _____
_____
_____

It is important to consider your worldwide opportunities from the start.

International Market

Our international strategy includes the following: _____
_____

List target countries in order of priority: rationale, language, usage of product.

_____
_____

Returns and Adjustments Policy

At this time, general trade customs for handling returns are [*describe how returns are generally handled*] _____

_____

_____.

We intend to [*follow/depart from*] _____ industry custom by implementing a returns and adjustments policy whereby [*explain your plan and how it will work*] _____

_____

_____.

Our reasons for [*following/departing from*] _____ customary procedures are [*give reasons—advantages, benefits for you and your customers*]

_____

_____

_____.

Remember: Promotion is an investment, not a cost.

Promotion

[*Company*] _____ recognizes the key to success at this time requires extensive promotion.   To accomplish our sales goals, we require an extremely capable advertising agency and public relations firm. Upon funding, an agency shall be selected and, with their assistance, a comprehensive advertising and promotion plan will be drafted. Advertising will be done independently and cooperatively with Distributors, OEM's, retailers and companies with whom [*Company*] _____ has joint marketing/sales relationships.

Describe how your advertising/ promotion objectives fit together to maximize the impact of your overall promotional campaign.

Objectives

Position [*Company*] _____ as the leading [*maker, servicer*] _____ in the market.

Your purpose: Enhance, promote, and support the fact that your products perform better.

Increase company awareness and brand name recognition among business managers and _____ retailers, buyers, customers.

Generate qualified sales leads and potential new distributors for field sales organization.

Develop, through market research, significant information to create immediate and long-term marketing plans.

Create product advertising programs supporting the [better taste, lower fat, more fun] _____ position.

Coordinate sales literature, demonstration materials, telemarketing programs and direct-response promotions in order to _____ _____.

Media Objectives

Gain awareness of company among industry groups, engineers, buyers, and customers and owners.

Establish an image of [Company] _____ as an organization that is professional, completely reliable and highly positioned in the market.

Maximize efficiency in selection and scheduling of published ads in publications to cover _____ and _____ markets.

Media Strategy

Select primary publications with high specific market penetration.

Schedule adequate frequency of ads to impact market with corporate image and product messages.

Where possible, position advertising in or near [articles on industry, product reviews, front cover, center spread] _____ and appropriate editorials.

Utilize U.S. editions of [consumer, trade, specialty publications] _____.

Take advantage of special high-interest issues of major publications when possible.

Maximize ad life with monthly and weekly publications.

When describing your audience focus, recap your customer profile from the Market Analysis section.

Select a specific group that buys your product or service.

To get the most out of our promotional budget, our media coverage will be to focus on a _____ audience.

We will develop an advertising campaign built around [*product innovation, high-performance, competitive advantages*] _____ , beginning with a "who we are" statement and supporting it with ads that reinforce the _____ message. Additionally, we will develop a consistent reach and frequency throughout the year.

Due to the nature of our product, it is necessary to run [*full-page 4-color ads only/ quarter-page black-and-white ads*] _____ .

Advertising Campaign

The best way to reach our potential customers is to develop an intense advertising campaign promoting our basic premise—[*your selling basis, theme, position in market*] " _____ _____ . "

To [*maintain/establish*] _____ our _____ company image, the delivery and tone of our statements will be [*understated elegance, hard driving excitement, excellence, glamour, reality, slice-of-life*] _____ .

Ads will convey the look and feel of a [*describe your image*] _____ company.

Research indicates that [*direct mail, direct response, TV, radio*] _____ type of advertising has not yet been used by any of our competitors.

The consumer mindset, as described in Marketing Strategy, is _____ .

When describing what the consumer will do, specify actual consumer action—call your 800# and place their order using their credit card, call for a brochure, attend your trade show booth, etc.

Ideally, after becoming familiar with our product, the consumer will _____ _____ .

To eliminate the biggest objections to immediate action, our advertisements must address [known/anticipated objections, difficulties with product acceptance, how to own/use product immediately] _____ .

Being specific here will set the stage for developing appropriate ads.

Because [product] _____ is so [innovative/unique/etc.] _____, it is important to develop a promotional campaign that is consistent and easy to understand.

Accordingly, [Company] _____ has created a system of research and response to insure the maximum benefit from advertising dollars.

Make a chart like this one for each publication and other outlet.

Obtain a copy of Standard Rate and Data Sheet.

Preliminary Media Schedule

	Circulation	Budget	Ad Size
[Magazine, TV, Radio] _____	50,000	$1,500	1/4 Page
_____	450,000	$4,400	1/2 Page
Total _____	500,000	$5,900	3/4 Page

Example: 1/1000.

Anticipated Response: _____ responses at $_____ each.

We expect to achieve a reach of [total circulation/audience] _____, and to maintain that for a period of at least [months] _____ .

Due to the [seasonal, geographical, etc.] _____ nature of our audience, we plan to [how you will counter these issues] _____ _____ _____ .

In regard to competitor's advertising, it is necessary to _____ _____ .

Explain how your message will contrast with theirs.

What if they run similar ads?

Examples of other ways you will gain recognition include the use of trade programs (trade advertising for product) and press releases (if product is justifiably new and innovative).

Include budget and rationale.

See also Public Relations section.

Sales Promotion

In addition to standard advertising practices, we will gain considerable recognition through ....

[Product] .... has already been installed at [companies, customers, stores, government agencies] ....

Our products will be [placed/offered] .... in additional .... at substantial discounts.

The number of trade shows attended will be increased from .... to .... each year. These shows will be attended independently and with companies with which [Company] .... has joint marketing/ sales or OEM agreements.

Reports and papers will be published for trade journals and technical conferences.

[Product] .... will be displayed as a service in a [retail store, manufacturing, professional] .... environment—a showcase for [Company's] .... products and an ongoing [test, market test, product development, promotional] .... environment.

Consumers will be encouraged to [call 800#, clip the coupon, come to store, call for a demo] ....

We will also use incentives for our customers such as:

Consider the appropriate use of advertising specialties like coffee mugs, t-shirts, imprinted gifts and gadgets.

Describe any activities or plans you have in this area.

Direct Mail

In addition to using direct mail to distribute our products, we will exercise our direct customer communications through [example: product upgrades, information updates] .... , and [*example: creation of a quarterly newsletter*] _____

_____.

The direct mail objective is fully for profit.

List Management

Given the growing potential of [*example: channel alternatives to the retail store*]

_____, we are building our capabilities

in database marketing. We have brought our customer list in house for this first

phase, as we develop our database sophistication. Our registration cards and

periodic customer surveys will help us understand our customer, and measure

the success of our marketing, sales and product activities. Profile overlays or

other lists that we buy will fill in our awareness gaps. This in-house presence

will provide our sales and tech support teams with tools that streamline their

operations, while they update our customer knowledge on a daily basis. We

plan to develop [*a customer information system*] _____

_____ that will help us make sound decisions by

providing historical answers to the marketing questions we pose.

Corporate Capabilities Brochure

To portray [*Company*] _____ as the leading

supplier of state-of-the-art dynamic _____, we have

developed a company brochure, which is included in Supporting Documents.

Sales Support Collateral Materials

Letter of introduction; business plan (brief outline describing objectives, strategy, tactics to align resellers); questions and answers; etc.

[*Company*] _____ has developed a variety of collateral

materials to support our sales efforts. These items and their intended purposes

include:

Audio/video introductory tape; news releases (list appropriate ones); brochures, etc.

Sell [*Product*] _____

[*Bulleted list of items*] _____

_____

_____

Attract and Support Distributors

[*Bulleted list of items*] ....

....

....

....

Presentation binder, data sheets, price lists, etc.

Help Distributors Sell

[*Bulleted list of items*] ....

....

....

....

When figuring your advertising budget, ask yourself the following questions:

What is the optimum spending level for advertising and promotion?

Do the "heavy spenders" perform better?

What are your conclusions on spending for advertising in this category?

Advertising Budget

For the next _____ [*months/years*] _____ advertising and

promotion will require $[*figure about 10 to 20% of sales the first year*] _____ .

On an ongoing basis we will budget our advertising investment as _____ % of

total sales.

This figure is necessary because of [*the specific goals you must meet*] _____

....

....

....

Use the Advertising Budget section of the Marketing Budget spreadsheet (MKTBDGT.XLS) to determine your costs.

Our Spending versus Industry Average

	Our Spending	Industry Average
Advertising	....	....
Sales Promotion	....	....
Trade	....	....
Consumer	....	....
Other [*specify*] _____	....	....

Compared to industry average, we are investing [*more/less*] _____ in

[*Trade, Consumer, etc.*] _____ promotion because _____

....

....

....

Include some references to advertising suppliers: advertising agency, public relations agency, direct mail, mailing house, direct response firm, fulfillment house, graphic designer, display designer, packaging supplier, demonstrations (guides, literature), market research focus groups, sales literature/tools, marketing consultant, planning consultant, premium suppliers, telemarketers, direct response advertising firm, printers.

Use the Public Relations section of the Marketing Budget spreadsheet (MKTBDGT.XLS) to determine your costs.

Outside Advertising Suppliers

_____

_____

_____

_____

_____

Public Relations

Our publicity efforts are intended to accomplish the following:

Position [*Company*] _____ at the leading edge

in providing [*product for industry or market segment*] _____ .

Increase [*Company*] _____ reputation and [*name/brand*]

_____ recognition among [*managers/buyers/customers in*

prospective companies/industries/markets] _____ .

Communicate on a regular basis with three target publics:

[*Editors of major trade, business and local publications*] _____

_____ .

[*Key management personnel in the existing customer companies*] _____

_____ .

[*Organization of employees and sales representatives*] _____

_____ .

See *Bacon's Publicity Checker* at your local library for a directory of publications and editors who cover your industry.

Publicity Strategy

During 19_____ [*Company*] _____ will focus on

the following publicity strategies:

Develop a sustained public relations effort, with ongoing contact between key editors and top-level personnel.

Develop a regular and consistent product update program for the major target

media, keeping key editors abreast of _____ enhancements

and _____ new product introductions.

Develop an internal newsletter that can cover key sales successes, significant marketing and manufacturing events, technical support and product development stories. Internally, the newsletter would be targeted at all company personnel and sales representatives; externally the piece would be targeted at key customers and prospects.

Develop a minimum of _____ technical articles written by key executives or engineers to be placed in [*list publications*] _____, _____ and _____ within the next _____ months.

Establish contact with editorial staff for the purpose of being included in product "round-ups"—product comparisons in [*publications such as Consumer Reports*] _____, where competing products are compared. This exposure builds credibility and market acceptance.

Briefly describe the subjects you would cover in a company "backgrounder."

Produce a complete company backgrounder on [*Company*] _____ to be used as the primary public relations tool for all target media editorial contact. This will also be effective for inclusion in press kits, dealer kits and sales packages. The backgrounder would include sections on the following broad subjects:

[*Overview of the market: size/characteristics*] _____

_____

_____

[*The Market in 19____, present and future*] _____

_____

_____

[*The Company (history, management philosophy, brief sketches of top executives)*] _____

_____

[*The products; market niches*] _____

_____

Major Sales Announcement

Major contract agreements representing sales volumes of over $ _____ will be written up and released to selected media as soon as practical after the signing of papers. Ideally, these will be joint announcements. Concurrently, a shortened version of the release will be mailed to all internal and external sales organizations.

Include an 8" x10" black-and-white glossy photo of your product(s) or of an interesting demo of your service—editors are likely to pick up your news release sooner with a photo.

Press Release

[Company] _____ [is developing/will develop] _____ a series of press releases on the entire [product line/service area] _____. We [have prepared/will prepare] _____ press releases for each new product introduction, technical development, participation in a major event, [awards/recognition] _____ for [product/personnel excellence/performance, etc.] _____.

Editorial Visits

Over the next _____ months we will [host/invite] _____ the most influential reporters and editors from [publication and/or broadcast media names] _____ for a visit to [Company]_____. During the visit, each of the editors would receive a complete facility tour, product briefing and an opportunity to interview the chairman, president, product designer and marketing manager. If logistics or timing is a problem with the interviews, then these could possibly be arranged at the major trade shows.

Use the Trade Show section of the Marketing Budget spreadsheet (MKTBDGT.XLS) to determine your costs.

Trade Show

[Company] _____ has participated in three kinds of trade shows: 1) _____, 2)_____, and 3) _____. In the past, we have concentrated on shows geared to _____. Now that _____ _____,

it's time to expand our horizons to shows that _____ _____.

In [year] _____, instead of _____, [Company] _____ will concentrate on

Factors to consider: target audience of the show, geographic location (good mix of shows around the country), timeframe (preferably no more than one show a month), past experience (if any with the show), participation in someone else's booth, keeping your "influencer" shows going.

In deciding on the [Company] _____ plan for trade shows, the following factors have been taken into consideration:

_____

_____

_____

_____

_____

Based on the above considerations, these shows have been chosen for 19_____:

_____

_____

Internal/External Newsletter

We [currently/plan to] _____ produce [a four-page, black-and-white, 2-color/4-color] _____ newsletter to serve as an informational piece for internal personnel, the sales force and key customers. It includes sections covering each major department or organization within [Company] _____ and a message from the executive staff. It also highlights major developments, such as [successful customer applications/uses/installations, key sales stories, significant marketing events, and product development news] _____

_____

Part 3: Sales Plan

Part 3 assists you in completing a sales plan that can be regularly referred to as a roadmap by the people who make your sales happen. Your sales plan is the part of your marketing plan that deals most directly with generating revenues for your company. Your written sales plan will address goals that are driven by sales, such as revenues and sales expenses, profit levels, return on capital, and growth rates.

A sales plan will also determine how much of any product you produce during a given time period, which in turn will affect the price of production and what you will need to charge your customers. The sales plan will outline estimates of sales, prices, and expenses.

Chapter 16

Sales Forecasting

Your sales forecast is important not only for predicting revenues. It's also crucial to your purchasing department to know how much to purchase to make the right amount of goods.

Learning Objectives

After completing this chapter, you should be able to:

1. Understand how forecasts are accomplished

2. Perform forecasts of revenues and sales

3. Differentiate among forecasting techniques

Your sales forecast tells purchasing personnel when you expect to sell, what you expect to sell, and how much you expect to sell. Purchasing could then answer the following questions:

• Can we supply the demand that's forecast?

• Can we provide all of it, or just a part?

• In what timeframe and at what cost can we supply demand?

◼ The Art of Forecasting

You don't have to be a statistical forecaster to appreciate the blend of facts, statistical analysis, research, common sense, and intuitive "gut feeling" that it takes to create a good forecast. While statistical models can prove helpful, don't rely solely on them.

Professional forecasters use statistical methods, backlog, history, and input from sales and field personnel in coming up with a valid forecast. This includes some "seat-of-the-pants" guessing based on your insight into what the competition is planning and what consumers are likely to do in the future. It's a good idea to compare your forecast to your sales history. This will give you an idea if you're on the right track or way off the mark.

Forecast Your Revenues

Revenue forecasts estimate how much money you expect to earn through sales in a given period. Your total revenue forecast minus the total sales cost forecast equals your total expected sales profit for the given period. Your expected profit from sales of products will guide how much you can spend on running other aspects of your business.

■ Forecast Your Unit Sales

Unit sales forecasts help you come up with the revenue forecasts and tell you how much of and when to produce your product. If you are a service provider, your unit sales could be identified at billable hours. Just as with your revenue forecasts, you need to forecast unit sales for each of your products.

A unit forecast will help you order raw materials, schedule production, and inform your distributors about how much you'll supply them with, among other things. For services, the unit forecast can assist with your staffing projections and scheduling needs. Obviously, you want to come as close to the mark in this forecast as you can, so that you're able to satisfy demand without overproducing.

■ Forecasting Techniques

There are many different theories and ideas about how to forecast best, and even the best forecasters are wildly wrong at some point in their careers, which is why forecasting should be seen more as an art than a science. Below, we discuss a few forecasting techniques or approaches, none of which are mathematically based.

Sales Force Opinion

Many companies look to their sales force to provide their own estimates and forecasts. Salespeople often have a sense of how their product is doing or how sales in a particular territory are going. Make sure to consider your sales force's opinions in coming up with your sales forecast.

Executive Opinion

Another way of forecasting is to solicit executive opinions within your company. These people often have a good feel for your company as a whole and, with the right supporting numbers, can come up with reasonable sales forecasts. At some point in any forecasting process, you should seek executive opinion and input.

Expert Opinion

Some companies hire outside agencies or expert individuals to come up with forecasts. While expert opinion may be valuable input, it often lacks insight into your company, its culture, and trends. However, an expert can provide you with opinions, insights, and suggestions from an objective outside perspective. This input can help you solidify your sales forecast.

Direct Market Test

In direct market tests, you explicitly ask consumers to divulge their future purchasing plans. The information you gather from this sort of test can be valuable, but there's a high margin of error. Always compare your test results with past results and trends.

■ Sales Forecasting Checklist

✓ Have you gone back and compared your previous forecasts to your sales history?

✓ Do you know enough about what your competitors are up to? This information can help you develop accurate forecasts of your own.

✓ Have you prepared your revenue forecasts?

✓ Have you prepared your unit sales forecasts?

■ Review Questions

1. What should your sales forecast tell you?

2. Why is a statistical model not necessarily the best forecasting tool?

3. Name and briefly define four sales forecasting techniques.

■ Activities

1. Review your competitor analysis for competitors' actions that could impact your forecast.

2. Identify forecasting techniques that are appropriate for your company to use (whether or not these techniques are being used currently).

Chapter 17

Budget for Sales

Depending on how your company is set up, you may have a budget specifically for your sales operations, for all your marketing efforts, or a mixture. Regardless of how your company is set up, you should know how to budget for your sales activities.

 **Learning Objectives**

After completing this chapter, you should be able to:

1. Understand components that make up sales costs

2. Identify other sales expense components

Forecasting is a key element to budgeting for all of your company operations, including sales. Your sales budget should cover the costs of selling your product, but should reflect your revenue and unit sales forecasts so that all your costs are covered.

■ Consider Your Sales Costs

You must take many costs related to sales into account when forecasting revenues. If you forget to include some of your marketing activities, you won't paint an accurate picture of how much profit you should make. The subjects listed below are the most obvious costs of sales.

Salary or Commission Expense

If you have salespeople on fixed salaries, your salary expense will be simple to forecast, unless you have plans to drastically change your sales staff configuration. If you use a commission structure, it will be slightly more difficult to come up with a commission expense forecast. If you have a thorough sales forecast, divided up by products, you can base your commission expense forecast on those numbers. Take the number of units you expect to sell and multiply their price by the percentage commission your employees earn. Fortunately, if you use a commission structure, your expenses will rise proportionately to sales levels, so if your sales estimates are not met, your commission expenses will be lower.

■ Other Sales Expenses

Companies often forget that miscellaneous sales costs add up over time. Depending on your sales strategy, these costs will vary. You should, however, remember that you may spend money on sales meetings, car mileage, customer gifts, travel and entertainment, sales literature, incentives, and training. All these things should be included so you come up with a realistic figure for sales costs.

Administrative support is often overlooked because it often crosses department lines. You will surely need administrative support to run your sales operation, even if you use independent salespeople. These administrative costs relate to sales and should be taken into account as you come up with a total cost of sales.

■ Sales Budget Checklist

✓ Does your sales budget take into account the cost of selling your product? Does it also reflect your forecasts for revenue and unit sales?

✓ Have you included salaries and commissions when figuring the cost of sales?

✓ Have you included other items in your sales budget, such as sales meetings, sales literature, and incentives?

■ Review Questions

1. What is the most important element in budgeting for sales operations?

2. What are the primary sales-related costs you should take into account when forecasting revenues?

3. What other expenses might be associated with sales?

■ Activities

1. List your primary sales costs.

2. List other sales expenses.

Chapter 18

Manage Your Sales

Sales can be challenging, requiring people skills, product knowledge, patience, and tenacity. Those organizations and individuals who are truly successful at sales organize their efforts into an orderly system. They seek to minimize wasted time and effort while investing resources effectively to produce maximum return. By organizing sales efforts, sales planning is possible.

 **Learning Objectives**

After completing this chapter, you should be able to:

1. Set sales goals and strategies

2. Understand your sales force

3. Manage your sales force

4. Organize a sales department

5. Know the steps of the selling process

6. Differentiate among different sales techniques

The sales manager's basic job is to maximize sales at a reasonable cost, while also maximizing profits. The tasks include setting sales goals, structuring the sales force, and recruiting, training, motivating, and evaluating the sales force. Successfully managing sales operations can be difficult, but it is much easier if a clear management system is set up.

■ Setting Sales Goals

The goals you set for your sales operations will largely be based on what you forecast for the next time period. The goals you lay out will direct all of your sales efforts, and it's crucial that your sales force knows and understands the goals that have been set.

■ Your Sales Strategies

Part of your sales management entails coming up with overall sales strategies. You need to make some important decisions so your sales efforts run smoothly and are effective. Following are some of the points to consider in developing sales strategies.

What Types of Selling Do You Use?

Do you plan to use a direct sales force, indirect sales, or a combination of both? Consider what you know about your target market. Which strategy is likely to be the best to follow? Will you use high involvement selling, where the salesperson spends time with the potential customer to secure the sale, or is the product straightforward?

Who Will Sell?

It's a good idea to have a clear idea of the type of salesperson you want to hire. Whether you hire a direct sales force or independents, the better you know what image you want to portray and what skills you think will strengthen your selling chances, the better equipped you'll be to find the right people.

When Do You Sell?

Are there certain times of year that your sales increase or decrease? Do you have more customers at certain hours of the day? You should come up with strategies that address those factors so that you take full advantage of sales opportunities.

How Do You Sell?

Think ahead about the type of sales tools your sales force will use. Also, communicate any sales techniques you have found to be useful in selling your product.

How Do You Support Sales?

You need to create strategies to support your salespeople. Address issues of how much of certain goods to stock at any given time, how to reorder in the most efficient way possible, and how to get goods from another store to satisfy customer demand. If your salespeople are highly effective but you don't have the right items in stock, their efforts will be lost.

■ Do You Know Your Sales Force?

There are different types of salespeople, ranging from those who stand behind a cash register and ring up purchases (no active selling) to those who rely on great technical knowledge and expertise to convince people to buy the product. The performance and capability of the whole range of salespeople in your company is important. The following discussion of sales force is focused on salespeople who actively engage in selling to and finding new customers.

Salespeople usually perform several different activities that supplement their actual selling efforts. No salesperson spends eight or more hours a day purely on sales. The job of sales should include the following.

The Art of Selling and Communications

Your salespeople need to be effective at the art of selling. Your salespeople should present your product well, be equipped to answer questions, know how to negotiate if necessary, and know how to close a sale. Communication is the key to sales. Your salespeople must have excellent communication skills so they can clearly explain your product to potential customers and adjust their presentation to different audiences.

Collecting Information

For salespeople to be successful in active selling, they must know how and where to collect information about customers' needs and your competitors' products. Sales representatives should provide you with some of the most valuable data for your market analysis.

Providing Service

Your customers may look to the people who sold them your product to help if they have problems. Your salespeople should either satisfy the customers' service needs or refer them to the appropriate person. If they do make a referral, they should always follow up and make sure the service has been taken care of.

Cultivating and Maintaining Relationships

A large part of sales is cultivating and maintaining relationships. You need people who can sense when customers are pleased or dissatisfied and who can react to both of those states. Sometimes, customers prefer to avoid confrontation if they are unhappy and simply buy from someone else. Your salespeople must give those customers the feeling that they are in a relationship worth maintaining and that they can communicate their problems or desires. A strong customer base that is built this way can be a major asset to a company and should be sought.

■ Managing Your Sales Force

Many factors come into play to manage your sales force successfully. You need to find the right people, train them, motivate them, know what they are doing, and pay them. Following are some management issues you should consider.

Finding Qualified Salespeople

Finding qualified salespeople can be difficult, costly, and time consuming. The best way to make the search work for you is to clearly define what you're looking for in a salesperson. The more clearly you have those qualifications in your mind, the more quickly you'll be able to eliminate ill-suited candidates. It's to your benefit to get it right the first time.

Employee turnover costs companies millions of dollars each year to conduct new searches and train new employees. One of your goals should be to hire people who you think will stay on for a while at your company. Think of ways to make the job challenging and satisfying and make your employees want to stay.

Sales Training

Many companies hire salespeople and send them straight out into the market with the product and a customer contact list. In most cases, this leads to ineffective selling. Train your salespeople so that when they do begin to sell, they provide a positive company image and close sales. Training can also boost morale and show your employees that you care enough to make an investment in their future.

Although training can be costly, it's necessary. Depending on the range and scope of your product, you'll need different levels of training with different areas of emphasis. The type of training your sales force needs will also depend on whether you're selling to the final consumer or doing business-to-business sales. Businesses will probably need more information, both about the product and pricing structure, than the final consumer.

Some companies provide ongoing training for their sales force so that they continue to learn and improve their sales performance. While it may be difficult to allocate your budget dollars to training, it should be worthwhile in the long run.

Some issues you might want to address in your training sessions include company policies and procedures, your product, overall company goals and objectives, target market profile, competitor profile, and sales techniques.

Setting Sales Policies

Setting clear sales policies is the best way to avoid misunderstandings and make sure that your company is being represented in a uniform manner. All salespeople should know how to deal with dissatisfied customers, how to get customers more technical information if the salesperson doesn't have it on hand, and how to properly make sales and receive payment. Established sales policies keep procedures clear, prevent misunderstandings, and keep company performance consistent.

Accountability and Visibility

To maintain control of your sales force, you should set up a sales system that allows for accountability and visibility. Your salespeople should be responsible for their performance, and their actions should be visible to management.

Setting Sales Quotas

Setting sales quotas is a common way that companies set goals for salespeople and measure their performance. Often, companies tie salaries or commissions to sales quotas. Companies take different approaches to setting sales quotas, with a variety of factors taken into account. The most important factor to consider is your sales forecast. Obviously, the minimum quotas you set need to add up to your projected sales for the year.

Controlling Your Sales Operations

It's a good idea to have control systems in place to monitor your sales efforts. A first step is to have sales representatives make regular reports of sales and progress towards quotas. You could also set up a process for salespeople to report any problems they have encountered or issues they think should be addressed immediately. Encourage salespeople to contribute in more ways than just selling, because they are likely to gain some valuable insight that you won't find anywhere else. If communication is not encouraged, that information may be lost.

Sales Compensation

You can choose from several options in deciding how to pay your sales force. You can also consider providing bonuses and covering sales costs. Once you have decided which type of selling will be most effective for your product, you can decide how you want to compensate your sales force.

Straight Salary

The straight salary option pays salespeople a fixed salary and expenses. Some of the advantages are that you have more control over your salespeople and can shift their duties with relative ease. It's also easier to forecast your costs if you pay straight salaries. Many people prefer to have a fixed salary for stability, and you may have higher employee morale using this method.

Straight Commission

On straight commission, your sales force is paid strictly as a percentage of sales. You may decide to pay your salespeople a percentage of the total revenue they bring in, a percentage of net profits, or by another method. With this method, salespeople are usually highly motivated. Every sale they make increases their income, so they put their maximum effort into selling your product. Your company also has no fixed costs related to the sales force; incomes will rise only if sales do.

Combination of Salary and Commission

This is the approach many companies take, because it usually offers the advantages of both of the above approaches and minimizes the disadvantages. In this approach, companies provide salespeople with a fixed salary that is lower than what they would receive in a straight salary setup and that they can increase through commissions. Your company has some fixed costs, although they are lower than if you offered a salary, and your company has more control over nonselling related tasks such as writing reports. Salespeople are still motivated to sell as much as possible with this method, because their level of sales has a direct impact on their final salary. In slow economic times, salespeople paid with this combination approach are more likely to stick around because they still receive some salary.

Bonuses

Bonuses are not a direct form of compensation, but they can provide incentives to your sales force for activities that are not rewarded by commissions. Bonuses can reward strong performance, positive results, or timely action. You can use cash bonuses, goods, travel, or anything that will make your salespeople satisfied. A downside to bonus awards is that they often rely on management judgment and can leave questions of fairness in employees' minds. One way to prevent this problem is to come up with the most objective benchmarks possible. Bonuses should raise employee morale, not lower it.

Sales Expenditures

Other sales costs are related to compensation, such as travel, administrative costs, insurance benefits, and training. If you decide to cover any or all of these costs, you're in fact providing your salespeople with more compensation. Simply put, what you pay they don't. These costs make it more expensive to have an in-house sales force, and you need to take them into account when budgeting.

■ Organizing Your Sales Department

You must organize your sales department in a way that promotes maximum effectiveness. Companies organize their sales departments in many different ways, depending on what they sell, who they sell to, how large their sales force is, and what their company goals are. To organize your sales department, make the chain of command clear. Your salespeople and managers must know who they report to, who they are responsible for supervising, and who is responsible for making the ultimate decisions.

Sales Force Structure

By Product

You may assign salespeople to sell one or more specific products. Then, they know exactly what they are responsible for and the quotas for those products. This approach can be especially effective if your products are complicated and require a great deal of technical knowledge to sell. This is also a good approach if you have very diverse products that are sold to different markets.

This is not necessarily the best approach if your customers are likely to buy a wide range of your products. It's awkward if a customer wants to buy several products and must be referred to more than one person. You may also have duplicate travel and sales calls if different people represent different products.

By Market

This approach divides your sales force into sections that deal with different markets, industries, or customers. You may decide to have salespeople who deal only with corporate customers, others who deal with retail customers, and still others who deal with wholesalers. You may also have a product that is used by several different industries.

By Territory

Territorial organization assigns salespeople to cover specific geographic regions for your whole product line. One advantage of territorial organization is that you often limit travel when your salespeople stay within one region. Another advantage of this system is that your sales representatives get to know regions and create personal relationships with their customers. It's also clear exactly who is responsible for sales in a particular region, so if sales are strong, that person can be rewarded.

A disadvantage of territorial organization is that your salespeople need to learn your whole product line. If you have a wide or complicated technical product line, it may be difficult for your salespeople to sell effectively.

Complex Sales Force Organization

A complex sales force organization is a combination of the different organization methods to create even more specific sales areas. For example, someone might be product-territory oriented, meaning they are responsible for selling a specific product or group of products in a certain territory. Again, you need to figure out your sales goals and organize your sales force to reach those goals in the most time- and cost-efficient manner possible.

■ Stages of a Successful Sale

Prospecting Your Leads

Sales is all about consistently having enough people in your "sales pipeline" to generate the amount of sales you want and need. A crucial step in the selling process is identifying potential customers, also called prospecting, and generating customer leads. While companies sometimes provide their sales force with leads and customer names, salespeople should always be looking for new customers to expand the company's customer base.

Part of the prospecting process is finding out as much as possible about prospective customers so that you can gear your sales presentation to their needs. Information about prospective customers will help you decide the best way to approach the company or individual, through a personal visit, a letter, or a phone call, and when an appropriate time might be to make contact.

Qualifying Your Leads

Qualifying customer leads means that you determine how likely people are to become actual customers. The more qualified someone is as a potential customer, the more resources you should be willing to spend on them.

Making Contact

At some point in the sales process, you must make contact with your prospective client. The more you know about the company or individual you're approaching, and their needs or culture, the better prepared you'll be to make a sale.

It's important to remember that, in addition to wanting a sale, meeting a potential customer gives you the opportunity to learn more about that customer's needs. Don't be overbearing and go on and on about your own product. Encourage the customer to speak and ask questions. The more you listen, the better you'll be able to gear your sales effort to meet the customer's particular needs. People like to be listened to and will appreciate comments and questions you make in reaction to what they say.

It's always useful to bring along a demo or sample of your product. This gives customers a better sense of what you're talking about and they're also more likely to remember the product if they've seen it. Sales literature such as data sheets, brochures, or a video can also serve as reminders after you're gone. If you make a good impression and stick in the customer's mind, you have a good chance of making the sale.

Always Follow Up

Following up on visits and contact with prospective clients is almost as important as making the initial contact. Many people will not buy from you after the first contact. Even if they do, you should still follow up on your visit.

You may send a thank-you letter, you may send a letter with information you promised to send, you may phone to ask if there are any more questions, or you may call to set up another meeting. While you'll need to decide on the most appropriate follow-up, there should be no doubt that some follow-up is crucial.

A lead that is not followed up is a lead wasted, and there is no room for waste in running a successful business.

Sales Techniques

In choosing sales techniques, you must consider your budget and your product. Does your product require personal selling or will direct mail do the job?

Personal Selling

Personal selling involves direct contact with the customer. Personal selling can be one of the most effective ways of selling because you have an opportunity to directly sway the consumer. It can also be one of the most expensive sales techniques because it requires more employees, travel, and other expenses. But personal selling can be an especially worthwhile investment when you're dealing with large clients, because a sale to them can mean a good return on the investment you've made in the sales force.

You have the choice to hire an in-house sales force or use independent sales representatives. If you choose independent representatives, you'll have lower expenses but less control over how your company and its products are represented. If a sales representative is unprofessional or chooses to emphasize another company's product that brings in more income, the sales and reputation of your business could suffer. With an in-house sales force, you have increased expenses for employee salaries and benefits such as Social Security taxes, pensions, and health insurance.

Cold Calling

A salesperson conducts a cold call when they try to speak on the phone or try to meet with someone who hasn't first expressed interest in your product or knowledge of it. Cold calls have a bad reputation; many people simply hang up the phone or close the door before you can finish or even start your sales pitch. According to Jeffrey Gitomer, author of *The Sales Bible*, your opening line is very important because it sets the tone for the whole interaction. If you turn someone off in the first instant, that sale is probably lost.

Cold calling is not a sales channel, it's an approach. While cold calling is by nature risky, in the sense that you have no solid indication the person you're calling may buy your product, many companies find it useful. You can improve your chances of success in cold calls by first qualifying your leads in some manner. Even if you don't make a sale during a cold call, obtain as much useful information about the customer as possible.

Maintaining Cost Efficiency

Cost efficiency is crucial to determining the success of your sales. If you use a method that generates a large volume of sales but is very expensive, it may not be worthwhile. Selling a lower volume of goods at a higher return may be a better approach. Compare your return on different sales methods to see which are the most cost efficient. Take into account your overall goals, because maybe you would accept a lower return to gain more market share.

■ Automate Your Sales

Sales automation allows salespeople better access to information about customers and markets, reduces the amount of paperwork involved in sales, and makes reporting simpler. The most common form of sales automation uses computers, including mobile laptop computers. Companies often look for ways to lower the cost of sales and to make the exchange of company wide information more fluid. Sales automation is one way to potentially reach both goals.

Choosing the Right Sales Automation Package

A variety of sales automation packages are on the market. You must consider what you want the package to do and find one that will meet your needs. If no package meets your needs, you may need to custom-design your own.

One popular sales automation technology, used by small and large businesses alike, is electronic data interchange (EDI). EDI allows companies to place orders with suppliers and vendors, and reduces the time needed to process orders by at least 25 percent. EDI also makes customer orders more accurate and allows companies to maintain smaller inventories without compromising customer service.

Benefits

As mentioned above, there are two main benefits of using a sales automation system in your company: (1) you save money, and (2) more and better information is exchanged. Remember, however, that simply purchasing and setting up a sales automation system in your company may not be enough. Salespeople must be trained on the system and must be receptive to using it or you won't benefit from it at all.

You can potentially save a great deal of money, because salespeople will spend less time filling out reports, trying to locate information, relying on administrative support, and even traveling. If your salespeople have laptop computers with them, they can have access to information in their computer or at the home office through network hookups. Thus, they have access to up-to-date information at all times and can check the most current customer information before meetings. They can also fill out reports as they go and provide that information to headquarters quickly. This allows greater information flow within your company and should allow you to react more quickly to changes in the market.

Costs

As with anything new, there are costs to incorporating sales automation into your company's structure. First, you'll have to buy equipment, both hardware and software. Then, you'll have to train your sales force on how to use the system effectively. Finally, you need to factor ongoing maintenance and enhancement of your sales automation system into your budget. Of course, a sales automation system is an investment in your company. The point is to cover all the costs of implementation and more in the long run.

■ Sales Management Checklist

✓ Does your company have someone who thoroughly understands your sales process?

✓ Have you set reasonable sales goals?

✓ In developing your sales strategy, have you considered issues such as your target market, the ideal salesperson, sales tools, special sales opportunities for your product, and selling techniques?

✓ Do you have a structure in place for managing your sales force?

✓ Do you provide adequate sales training?

✓ Do you have clear sales policies? For example, does your entire sales force know how to deal with dissatisfied customers?

✓ Are your salespeople accountable and visible?

✓ Do you have adequate control systems in place to monitor your sales effort and make sure you're heading in the right direction?

✓ Do you have good communication with your sales force on issues such as sales expectations and compensation?

✓ Is your sales department organized effectively to maximize sales?

✓ Do you have a good process in place for generating customer leads? Do you take the time and effort to qualify leads?

✓ Have you stressed the importance of follow-up with your sales force?

✓ Do you take advantage of the most effective techniques for selling your product?

✓ Does your sales automation package meet your needs?

■ Review Questions

1. What are some important factors to consider when setting sales strategies?

2. What does the job of selling entail?

3. Evaluate the different methods of compensating the sales force.

4. What are some ways of structuring the sales force? Under which conditions does each structure work best?

5. List the stages of a successful selling process.

6. Discuss different selling techniques, including sales automation.

■ Activities

1. Set goals for your sales operations.

2. Decide on overall sales strategies. In particular, consider the advantages and disadvantages of using an outside, independent sales force versus your own.

3. Set sales quotas.

4. Decide how to organize your sales force. Is this structure the most suitable for your firm and its products?

5. Outline specifics of a sales presentation for your firm's product or service. This outline could be used in a training session.

6. Complete the following portions of the Sales Plan template (3-SALES.DOC): Sales Strategy, Positioning, Pricing, Margin Structure, Current Selling Methods, Marketing Responsibilities, and Next Steps.

Chapter 19

Sales and Distribution Channels

Sales and distribution channels are the different outlets through which you can sell your product. You can use many different channels, including retail, wholesale, and direct mail; you may use one channel or a variety of channels. The importance of choosing the right channel is to reach the maximum number of potential customers in an effective manner.

 *Learning Objectives*

After completing this chapter, you should be able to:

1. Choose an appropriate channel and select the best marketing method for that channel

2. Decide on your sales strategy or distribution intensity

3. Select which type(s) of selling channels to use

4. Understand vertical integration

5. Know channel pricing and promotional strategies

6. Recognize sales approaches in the introduction stage of the product life cycle

7. Evaluate distribution

■ Choosing Channels

Sales or distribution channels are the different avenues through which you can sell your products. You need to decide on the best way to get your product to a place where a potential customer will see it and buy it. The channels through which you decide to sell your product will influence other marketing and company-wide decisions. You should take into account a number of factors when deciding which sales channels to use.

Price

How will the channel you use affect the price you can charge? For example, if you sell to a wholesaler or a large retail chain, you'll have to charge a lower per-unit price than if you sell in your own retail outlet.

Perception

How do you want your product to be perceived? Where you sell will influence the perception your prospective customers have of your product. If you sell your product at an exclusive boutique, consumers might assume it's good quality.

Constraints

What constraints will affect your ability to use certain channels? If you're selling produce, for example, you have a limited time to get it to market because it's perishable. It may be easiest to distribute the produce yourself or have one trusted distributor. If your product is unusually large or heavy, you would want to limit the distance it would need to go to market. If your product needs a lot of explaining, you may decide to use only a few retail outlets with the demonstrated expertise to sell your product. You would probably not want to use an intermediary who could not devote the time to understanding your product.

Competitors

What channels are your competitors using? You may or may not want to sell your product through the same channels as your competitors. You should carefully consider the consequences of choosing the same channels. Is it important that you have a presence in the retail outlets where your competitors sell? Or, do you want to sell in the same places, while also looking for new, untapped channels? If your main competitors' products are sold mostly through retail channels, maybe you should sell retail and also set up a mail-order branch.

Ease of Administration

How easy is it to administer your distribution system? While you might achieve the highest sales levels by distributing your product through 20 different channels, you may simply not be able to do that. How many sales channels can your company realistically manage efficiently? You can always expand your distribution network, so you should not be overzealous about using every possible sales channel.

■ Marketing Methods

The decisions you make about your target market will influence which channels you decide to use. In choosing the channel, your company's goals play a part as well. Do you want to have total control over your products and sell them directly to your customers, either in your own stores or by mail, or do you want to reach as many people as possible and not worry about sales on that level? Below are some approaches you might decide to take.

Sell to Everyone

This first strategy is the most broad; you simply try to sell to everyone. Although this may sound like the way to make the most sales, it's usually an unrealistic approach. Consumers have different wants and needs, and each group needs to be solicited with a message specifically aimed at them. If you were truly to sell to everyone, you would have to reach an extremely broad range of groups, which would probably be impossible.

Differentiated Marketing

This method attempts to modify your marketing and sales strategies so that you can reach two or more segments. If you use this approach, you could sell your product in a variety of channels, in different geographic locations, or with different demographic characteristics. However, you may need to tailor aspects of your product, price, promotion, and distribution to these different groups.

Concentrated Marketing

The most limited type of segmentation is called concentrated marketing. In this approach, you select one target segment or a few closely related target segments. It's important to remember that people will make the final buying decision based on how they perceive your product. Those perceptions are grounded in their personal emotional state and how they view themselves. It's not enough for your product to be the cheapest, the best, or the most available; it must be perceived as the socially correct one. If you use this approach, you'll distribute your product through a limited number of highly selected channels.

■ Sales Strategies

Sell Everywhere You Can

Often described as the "shotgun" approach, this extensive approach to distribution sells your product through as many retailers as possible without regard to image or competition. The idea is to sell through all possible outlets where the customer would expect to find your product.

Sell Selectively

Selective distribution is the broad category between extensive selling and exclusive selling. The aim of selective distribution is to reach as many potential customers through as many outlets as possible, while maintaining some type of image. There is no need to sell your product through *every* retail outlet under this distribution strategy.

Be Exclusive

Exclusive distribution, often called the "rifle approach," is selling your product at a very limited number of retail outlets, either a single store or chain or in a limited georgraphic area. The objective of exclusive distribution is to reach a single target market. Usually, strong dealer loyalty and active sales support from the dealer are necessary to make this approach work. Exclusive distribution is brand and image conscious and is usually used in conjunction with a concentrated marketing strategy. In choosing this distribution strategy, it's important to avoid distributing to competing channels.

■ Sales Channels

Retail

Retail selling in your own store is selling goods or services directly to consumers for their own personal use. Retail can be an expensive and complicated way to sell your goods because you may need storage space, and you'll definitely need more employees. While this may be more expensive, it can also be more profitable because you cut out the intermediaries who take a cut of your sales. You won't have to lower your price for a wholesaler or distributor, and you'll have more control over how your product is sold. Mail-order businesses take this a step further by getting away from the need for stores from which to sell their products.

Direct Mail

Direct mail can be considered a distinct sales channel because you can actually sell your product through the mail. One of the most common types of direct mail specifically designed to generate sales is the mail-order catalog. Catalogs can be an effective way to reach people because they usually have pictures; in many cases, they are almost magazine-like. Consumers don't feel imposed upon by this type of selling, because they enjoy looking at what you offer.

Catalogs are a good way to show consumers what they want and need, especially for luxury items they don't really need. Catalogs are a relatively effortless way for people to shop and impulse shop. In most cases, all consumers have to do is call a toll-free number, and give their credit card number. Within days, they receive their product.

Another type of direct mail that can effectively spur sales is making announcements through the mail. You may announce an upcoming sale or the arrival of a new shipment of special products. "Hurry In Before We're Sold Out Again!" In this type of direct mail, you want to get people to come to your store, so create a sense of urgency.

Telemarketing

Outbound

Telemarketing is personal selling over the phone. Many companies use telemarketing to reach a large number of customers for relatively low cost. One major problem with telemarketing is that its reputation is spotty. Many consumers simply hang up the phone if they hear that someone is trying to sell them something. In order to make telemarketing work for your company, you must prepare a strategy to keep customers on the phone. This method is called outbound telemarketing because your salespeople are making calls out of your location.

Inbound

Inbound telemarketing uses 800 and 900 numbers and solicits customers to call those numbers. Catalogs usually have 800 numbers for customers to place orders or ask questions, and many advertisements include an 800 number to call for more information or to place an order. This can be an effective way to generate leads and make sales.

Door-to-Door Sales

Door-to-door sales are a type of direct field sales. This type of selling has a mixed reputation, because many people do not like to be bothered at home. This method is better for selling to businesses.

Distributors

Distributors can be different people with different functions. They can be the trucking companies who physically distribute your product, or they can be intermediaries, such as wholesalers, who sell your product to retailers. Distributors can also be in charge of selling your products through different channels. Using distributors is a form of indirect sales because you have little or no contact with the end consumer.

Wholesalers

Wholesalers buy goods and services for resale or business use. Retailers often prefer to deal with one or two wholesalers instead of every individual vendor. They can then establish one or two strong relationships and cut down dramatically on the time it takes to buy.

If you manufacture a product and want to sell it through certain stores, they might require that you use a wholesaler. Dealing with wholesalers can also cut down on your time spent selling your product. Wholesalers will often buy a large amount of your product.

Original Equipment Manufacturer (OEM)

The OEM sale has the lowest cost and the highest real margin. OEM sales are selling your product, or a version of it, to an original equipment manufacturer, who includes your product with what they sell. This is sometimes called bundling and can be a way to gain wide market exposure and solid market penetration. OEMs will often bundle or promote your product with theirs or pay a royalty on each product sold.

Value Added Resellers (VARs)

A VAR develops customer loyalty by "adding value" to your product. A consultant is a good example of a VAR. A VAR does not make a product, but instead provides a service in addition to your product that is considered an extra value by the customer. If you develop close and personal relationships with VARs, as well as training, referrals, and regular communication, VARs can be a good choice for channel distribution.

Dealers

Dealers add value to your product by providing floor space and end user sales. Successful dealers prefer to buy from a wholesaler to minimize their vendor list. They want consolidated billing and dependable deliveries. Dealers want to buy products they will have little difficulty selling, so advertising and promoting your product will ensure dealer interest.

Franchises

Franchising allows someone to either sell your product as their own business or use your company name and setup. In a franchise agreement, the franchiser sells the franchisee the right to sell their product. Usually, the franchisee pays the franchiser an initial fee and then a percentage of gross sales annually. Some franchisers also take a percentage of revenues for advertising and promotion.

The advantage of franchising is that the franchising company receives increased earnings with little risk and minimal investment. People who run franchise businesses are usually motivated and ambitious enough to start a business, but the whole endeavor would be riskier for them on their own. Of course, you have to have brand name recognition and a unique concept to sell franchises successfully.

■ Vertical Integration

Vertical integration is one way that channels are managed. A vertical integration system means that the different players involved in manufacturing goods are linked to those who sell and distribute them. In a traditional channel distribution system, all players are out for themselves; the producer wants a maximum profit even if the retailer loses, and vice versa. Vertical integration brings those different forces together so that they work for a common good.

Vertical integration is definitely not for everyone. Usually, only large companies have the capital to buy the different components of their business. Vertical integration, however, does not necessarily mean that one company must own others. Companies can also come to mutually beneficial arrangements.

■ Channel Pricing

You'll most likely have to charge different prices in different distribution channels. This will mostly depend on the time and effort you save in actual selling. For example, you should charge wholesalers less because they buy your product up-front and you don't need to worry about sales to retail outlets or final consumers.

In deciding what price to charge different buyers, a commonly used strategy is to take the final price that you believe the end user should pay and adjust it accordingly for different channels. It's a good idea to come up with standard policies about how much to mark down (or mark up) prices for the various channels you're using. Remember, though, to keep some flexibility so that you don't eliminate deals that are not within your strict guidelines.

■ Promotional Expenditures

Some channel distributors will expect you to pay for sales promotions, even if they are selling out of their own retail outlet. You should be open to this option, as long as distributors are willing to explain exactly how they will spend your money and how they expect to increase sales of your product. Give your distributors some flexibility because, in many cases, they will have a better idea of how to reach the consumer than you do. If possible, ask for their sell-through numbers based on the specific sales promotions they run. Keep them accountable and effective to the extent that you have influence.

■ Launching New Products

The sales approaches you use during different periods of your product's life cycle are bound to be different. Launching a new product is probably the most crucial point for making sales work. If you do not achieve a reasonable level of sales after the product is launched, you may have to discontinue it. While advertising and publicity are very important in this stage, so are sales strategies.

You need to decide where the best place is to sell your product just after it's launched. This will depend on your company and how well it's known, whether the product is similar to other products you have, and how technologically advanced it is. If your product is completely new and not known by a majority of consumers, even those in your target group, you would probably want to sell your product through channels that aim at a small market, such as specialty stores that look for new and innovative products. You might expand to reach a broader audience and use more channels at a later time.

If you're a well-known company with high brand recognition, you may decide to sell the product through your normal channels, and just place some extra emphasis on sales promotions, personal selling, and advertising for the product in the initial stage.

■ Evaluating Distribution

Once companies have created distribution systems, many of them just sit back and stick with that setup. On a regular basis, you should evaluate your distribution system. Maybe you could sell more of your product if you include more channels, or maybe one of your current distributors is not successfully placing your product on the market.

■ Sales and Distribution Channels Checklist

✓ Have you taken the appropriate factors into account in selecting your sales channels—your product's price, how you want it to be perceived, which sales channels the competition uses, and so on?

✓ What is your market segmentation strategy—sell to everyone, differentiated marketing, or concentrated marketing?

✓ What sales strategy have you adopted—sell everywhere, sell selectively, or be exclusive?

✓ Are you making use of all the appropriate sales channels—retail, direct mail, telemarketing, distributors, wholesalers, OEMs, VARs, dealers, and franchises?

✓ Have you looked at your selling costs in each sales channel and adjusted your prices accordingly? You should have standard policies for how much to mark up or down in each channel.

✓ Have you developed a sales strategy for launching a new product?

✓ Do you evaluate your distribution system periodically?

■ Review Questions

1. What are the factors you should consider when choosing a distribution channel?

2. You have three basic choices for distribution intensity. What are they, and what sorts of products are distributed with each method?

3. List sales channel alternatives that use an intermediary. Then list sales channel alternatives that require different selling methods.

4. What is vertical integration? Is it right for your company?

5. Discuss aspects of channel pricing and channel promotions.

6. How can a sales approach help launch a new product?

■ Activities

1. Choose channels and sales strategies for your firm's products. Use the Distribution Channels portion of the Sales Plan template (3-SALES.DOC) to assist you.

2. Select which particular channels you can feasibly utilize. Use the Distributors, Retailers, OEMs, Direct Response Mail, Telemarketing, International Market, and Method of Distribution portions of the Sales Plan template (3-SALES.DOC) to assist you.

3. Select a distribution intensity level for your firm's product. Use the Coverage portion of the Sales Plan template (3-SALES.DOC) to assist you.

4. Delineate distribution strategies for a new product launch, if appropriate for your company. Use the Product Roll-Out Program portion of the Sales Plan template (3-SALES.DOC) to assist you.

3-SALES.DOC

It is important to address how long before the product pays for itself.

Briefly discuss how your sales strategy will address specific market/ environmental conditions.

Sales Strategy

Because of [product's] _____ special market characteristics, [seasonal/geographic/etc., as mentioned in Market Analysis]

_____ ,

our sales strategy [includes/incorporates] _____ :

_____

_____

_____

_____ .

How do you set prices? Is there a policy?

Is there perceived value (it costs more, therefore it must be better) inherent in higher prices?

Are prices based on costs (standard markup)?

Why are they higher or lower than competing prices?

How elastic (effect of pricing on demand) is the market for these products? How does consumer preference affect elasticity?

Pricing

The prices for our products are determined first and foremost by [competition/ costs/suppliers/manufacturers/package deals] _____ .

It is important to know that [sliding scales/volume/regulated/competitive/perceived value] _____ pricing is essential to our market profile.

List examples of competitive pricing.

Include copies of price comparisons and reports as attachments.

Compared to the competition, our prices are _____ .

Different seasonal aspects of our market affect our pricing because [example: selling seasons] _____

_____ .

We feel that our customers will pay $_____ because [purchasing rationale]

_____

_____

_____ .

Ask friends and customers in retail management about quantities they are likely to buy. What discounts would entice them to order more?

Margin Structure

Retail

_____

_____

Ask about quantities their customers are likely to order and their Gross Profit Margins/Percentages.

Distributor

_____

_____

What percentage commissions do they make (usually between 5 and 20%)?

Manufacturer's Representative

_____

_____

Determine cost of each sale—time and expense involved, package deals.

Direct Sales

_____

_____

Discounts

Volume discount is applicable for scheduled orders. Discounts for paying cash or paying within a certain number of days?

We can take advantage of volume purchases by _____

_____

_____

_____

We plan to review our pricing and product/service margin every _____ months.

Should a new pricing policy be investigated? Are potential profits being lost?

Current Selling Methods

We currently use [activities used in selling your product or service] _____

Describe the activities used in selling your product or service.

_____

_____

_____

to sell [product] _____

Describe methods you use to promote product or service: direct calling, telephone, advertising, mail, radio, television, etc.

Methods we use to promote [*product*] _____ include _____

_____

_____

_____

Place sample brochure or dummy, advertisements, announcements, or other promotional literature in the Supporting Documents section.

Remember that margins of safety are allowed in sales forecasts.

Next Steps

Based on the strategic plan, decisions that must be made now include _____

_____

_____

Data, research results, etc.

The information needed to make those decisions is _____

_____

Also, discuss decisions to be made before the next fiscal budgeting process.

Key decisions to be made in the [*near term/next six months*] _____ are

_____

_____

Include primary research projects (topic, timeframe, budget) and secondary research studies (topic, vendor, timeframe, cost).

The information needed to make both of these decisions with confidence includes _____

_____

_____

_____

List questions you need immediate answers to.

The most sensible research recommendations are to _____

_____

_____

Types of determining factors are customer profile, geography, seasonal variations, efficient use of funds, and feasibility of using channels of similar products already on the market.

Distribution Channels

[Company's] _____ marketing department plans to sell our [product] _____ through several channels.

The determining factors in choosing these channels are _____
_____
_____ .

Key competition uses the same _____ distribution channels. Our mix of distribution channels will give us the advantages of [list advantages] _____
_____
_____

over our competition.

List the top 5 to 10 customers.

A partial list of [Company's] _____ major current customers includes: _____
_____
_____
_____ .

This type of selling is usually most appropriate for very expensive products or services (executive jets, yachts, large estates) where it is important to deal principal to principal when negotiating the sale.

Executive Sales

Because our customers tend to be top corporate managers, it is important that our company president and senior managers present our product to our customers.

Direct Sales

The majority of [Company] _____ sales will be handled internally through direct sales by our staff.

[Company] _____ anticipates hiring _____ additional sales representatives to [cover additional territories/retailers/distributors/ markets/sell specific products] _____
_____ .

We have chosen to use a direct sales force because our products require considerable customer education and post-sales support—directly from the company. Our price point, pricing structure, and profits are such that our costs of sales warrants "person-to-person" selling strategy.

Manufacturers' Representatives

Contact customers and retailers and ask them who they would recommend to represent your product (firms and people they respect and use).

Because manufacturers' representatives carry several product lines that are compatible with ours, we feel that it would be appropriate to select manufacturers' representatives carrying .... , and [*complementary and compatible products—automotive products to parts stores, marine supplies to boat dealerships, etc.*] ....

....

We would also select manufacturers selling [*dissimilar products yet appropriate to their customers' customer—publishers selling computer software to bookstores, etc.*]...............................

....

Distributors

Distributors must mark up your prices 15-30% to their retailers. Your sales revenue will have to be reduced in order to allow distributors their profit margin.

Consider using advertising and direct mail to locate appropriate distributors.

One of the key elements designed into the [Company] .... marketing plan is the targeting of our distributors. We will select distribution channels already in existence and staffed with professionals possessing appropriate backgrounds and clientele.

[Company]'s .... products are very pertinent to the nature of the distributor's business and to the well-being of their customer base. Also, it is significantly less difficult for us to reach these people and educate them about the benefits available in using [*product*] ....

This strategic marketing approach takes full advantage of the fact that these professionals are already involved with parallel products and services. They already have a track record of experience.

By operating within these distribution channels in this manner, we can maintain control of our market. In addition, we can generate growth at a reasonable pace and obtain excellent sales results.

List any national or regional chains or independent stores that could carry your product.

Retailers

Possible retail and wholesale outlets include: _____

_____

_____ .

OEMs

With Original Equipment Manufacturers (OEMs), we can incorporate our

[*product*] _____ into their product line by [*explain*

how your product can be included within theirs—they sell your outboards with their boats, your

windshield wipers with their cars] _____

_____

_____ .

For manufacturers of [*their biggest system/product*] _____ ,

we can sell [*product*] _____ as part of their

_____ .

We can also provide a private-label line as an additional product for

_____ distributors.

Telemarketing

We will use an [*in-house/contract*] _____ telemarketing service to

perform the following functions.

Literature mailing, follow-up calls, order entry, etc.

Provide outside sales support by _____

_____

Order entry, literature mailing, 800# order/support hotline, marketing research, etc.

Respond to inquiries by _____

_____

Contact distributors, retailers, customers; schedule appointments; etc.

Generate new business by _____

_____

_____

Make a chart to show how products get to the end-user consumer.

Method of Distribution

The primary means of distribution will be ....

....

....

Additional channels planned are ....

....

....

An important advantage to these alternate channels is flexibility.

By using more than one method, [Company] ....
will have more control and be better able to respond to special needs and circumstances.

Coverage

Regional target areas are [where you will begin sales] ....

....

Reports indicate that these areas generate the highest level of consumer interest.

Because our distribution network is [already set up or in use/easy to implement/cost-efficient, etc.] ....,
we can enjoy [national/international] .... delivery immediately. This, in turn, will reduce shipping time and increase customer satisfaction.

To date, [many of, ... of, none of] .... our competitors [are/is] ....
able to achieve this.

Who or what markets can generate business immediately? Who might be easiest to identify and who would be closest your target?

Product Roll-out Program

For first entry into the market, the specific market areas we have selected are [list key roll-out market areas and activities] ....

....

....

....

With these customers, you can refine your program and generate some inexpensive initial business before you expand to your next level of markets.

After initial roll-out and evaluation of the results, we will expand our marketing to additional market areas in this order of priority: [*list additional market areas for intended penetration*] ....

....

....

....

....

List and describe regions or market areas in order of roll-out sequence.

List key distributors, retailers, etc., in support of each of the top priority areas.

In support of this program, Manufacturers' Representatives we have chosen are:

Name	Territory	Type

Distributors we have chosen are:

Name	Customer Base	Type

Retailers we have chosen are:

Name	Number of Outlets	Type

There are [*number*] .... of [*retailers/dealers*] .... in each region who we will work with and support to insure the success of our roll-out program.

Customer Service

Our customers emphasize that service and support is one of their major concerns. They are constantly impressed with the support we provide. Hot-line service is currently available to all customers enrolled in a maintenance/support program.

We intend to provide free pickup and delivery for customers in the _____ areas by using [our own trucks/couriers] _____ .
The purpose for this service is to assure customer satisfaction and loyalty, allowing us to increase sales as well as maintaining a high profile within our service area.

Another service to add value is to provide warehousing of customer inventory. This allows us to book larger orders and provide faster order response.

Support to manufacturers' representatives will allow them to perform efficiently as a sales force. We intend to treat the manufacturers' representatives as an extension of the [Company] _____ direct sales force, and they will be given the same support as the [Company] _____ internal sales staff.

Technical backup to OEM support groups is currently supplemented by [Company] _____ . The OEM staffs respond to the needs of their customers, and when they encounter a support issue that requires more information, they may direct their customer to [Company] _____ or they may contact [Company] _____ to obtain the necessary information.

Technical support to marketing and sales functions will be strengthened. Pre- and post-sales situations involving the application, presentation, and demonstration of [products] _____ will be supported by [staff] _____ .

Returns and Adjustments Policy

At this time, general trade customs for handling returns are [*describe how returns are generally handled*] ....

....

....

We will use the following policies:

"If for some reason [*product*] .... is not right for your business, you may return it for a full refund within 30 days of receipt of product. You must call [*phone number*] .... for a Return Authorization number [*RA#*] .... Refunds are made only on the price of the package plus applicable taxes and do NOT include shipping costs."

"Credit card refunds are credited to your account and cash/check payments are refunded within 30 days of receipt of returned merchandise in good condition with RA#."

We intend to [*follow/depart from*] .... industry custom by implementing a returns and adjustments policy whereby [*explain your plan and how it will work*] ....

....

....

Our reasons for [*following/departing from*] .... customary procedures are [*give reasons—advantages, benefits for you and your customers*]

....

....

Appendix A

Using MarketingBuilder Express

Appendix A will help you install MarketingBuilder *Express* quickly and easily. It covers these topics:

- What You Need to Use MarketingBuilder *Express*
- What's On the MarketingBuilder *Express* Disk
- File Compatibility
- Installing MarketingBuilder *Express*

For technical support using the MarketingBuilder *Express* files, call South-Western College Publishing at 1-800-543-0174.

■ What You Need to Use MarketingBuilder *Express*

You need the following equipment and software to install and use MarketingBuilder *Express*:

- An IBM-compatible 286 PC or higher with:
  - 4 MB RAM
  - 2 MB free hard disk space
  - 3.5" high-density floppy disk drive
  - Windows 3.1 or Windows 95
- Word processing software (see p. 255)

■ What's On the MarketingBuilder *Express* Disk

Your MarketingBuilder *Express* disk contains word processing template files to assist you in your sales and marketing efforts.

Market Analysis	1-MKTANL
Marketing Communications	2-MARCOM
Sales Plan	3-SALES
Top 20 Questions	QUESTION

Depending on which format you select during installation, the files have the extension .DOC or .RTF.

■ File Compatibility

The MarketingBuilder *Express* files are supplied in two formats:

- Microsoft Word 2.0 for Windows (.DOC)

- RTF (Rich Text Format) - used for transferring formatted text documents between applications and between platforms (.RTF)

The following table lists several of the most popular PC word processors, and shows our recommendation for the MarketingBuilder *Express* file format that will work best with those word processors. This is the file format that you should specify during the installation process.

If your word processor is:	Select this option:	To install text file templates in this format:
Ami Pro 3.0 & 3.1 for Windows	1	Word 2.0 for Windows
Claris Works 1.0 and later (Windows)	1	Word 2.0 for Windows
FrameMaker 3.0 and Later	1	Word 2.0 for Windows
Microsoft Word 2.0 and later (Windows)	1	Word 2.0 for Windows
Microsoft Works 2.0 and later (Windows)	1	Word 2.0 for Windows
Ami Pro 2.0 for Windows	2	RTF
WordStar 6.0, 7.0	2	RTF

■ Installing MarketingBuilder *Express*

Important: Since MarketingBuilder *Express* is a set of files and not a software application, the Setup program cannot create a MarketingBuilder *Express* Windows program group or icon. The MarketingBuilder *Express* files are simply installed on your hard drive in a directory named MBEXPRS (or whatever directory name you specified during the setup procedure) and may now be accessed through your word processor.

If your hard drive is something other than C and/or your floppy disk drive is something other than A, use the correct letter in place of C and/or A in these instructions.

1. Insert the MarketingBuilder *Express* disk into the floppy disk drive.

Windows 95 Installation

2. Click on the Start button, then select Run.

3. From the Open Command line, type A:\SETUP and click OK. In a few moments, the Welcome to JIAN! window displays. Click OK when you are ready to continue. Go to step 4.

Windows 3.1 Installation

2. From the Windows Program Manager, select File, then select Run.

3. In the Run window Command line, type A:\SETUP and click OK. In a few moments, the Welcome to JIAN! window displays. Click OK when you are ready to continue.

4. Select the option that lists the name and version of your word processor (See table on previous page.) Click OK.

5. Install creates a default installation directory, C:\MBEXPRS. You may specify a different hard drive or directory if you prefer. Click OK. The install program installs the templates in the directory you specified.

Removing MarketingBuilder Express

MarketingBuilder *Express* installs a program (UNSTALL.EXE) that allows you to remove MarketingBuilder *Express* from the hard drive or directory that you originally specified.

■ Using the .DOC Files

This section contains instructions for using the word processing templates with two of the most popular Windows-based word processors: Microsoft Word for Windows and Microsoft Works for Windows.

Microsoft Word 2.0 and 6.0 for Windows

The MarketingBuilder *Express* text files are Microsoft Word for Windows 2.0 files. You can open, edit, save, and print them as you normally would any Word for Windows document.

Follow these steps to open any of the MarketingBuilder *Express* .DOC files:

1. Start Microsoft Word for Windows.

2. Select File, then select Open.

3. In the Open window, double-click on C:\ in the Directories listing. Next, double-click on MBEXPRS. The MarketingBuilder *Express* text filenames appear in the Files box.

4. Select the .DOC file you want to open (for example, QUESTION.DOC). Word opens the file and displays it on the screen.

Microsoft Works 2.0 and 3.x for Windows

Follow these steps to convert the MarketingBuilder *Express* .DOC files to Microsoft Works for Windows format. After you convert the files, you can open, edit, save, and print them as you normally would any Microsoft Works document.

1. Start Microsoft Works for Windows.

2. Select File, then select Open Existing File.

   Version 3.0 Users: Click the Open Existing File icon on the opening window.

3. On the Open menu, double-click C:\ in the Directories box. Next, double-click on MBEXPRS.

4. Under List File of Type at the bottom left corner of the window, click on the down arrow key to scroll through the options and select Word 2.0 for Windows. The File Name scroll box now displays a list of MarketingBuilder *Express* .DOC files.

5. Select the file you want to open (for example, QUESTION.DOC), then click OK. Works converts the file into its internal format and displays it on the screen.

6. Select File, then select Save As. Make sure the Save File As Type option is set to Works WP.

7. Change the filename extension from .DOC to .WPS, then press Enter.

8. Select File, then select Close.

To retrieve one of the newly converted MarketingBuilder *Express* .WPS files, follow steps 2 and 3 above. Make sure the List Files of Type box displays Works WP (*.WPS), then select the MarketingBuilder *Express* .WPS file you want to work with from the File Name scroll box.

Appendix B

Resources

Government Agencies

Federal Government

Bureau of Labor Statistics
2 Massachusetts Ave. NE
Washington, DC 20212
202-606-5902

Congressional Budget Office
402 Ford Bldg.
2nd and D Sts. SW
Washington, DC 20515
202-226-2600

Consumer Product Safety Commission
Washington, DC 20207
310-504-0580

Economic Development
Administration
14th St. and Constitution Ave. NW
Washington, DC 20230
202-482-5112

Employment and Training
Administration
200 Constitution Ave. NW
Washington, DC 20210
202-219-6871

Employment Standards Administration
200 Constitution Ave. NW
Washington, DC 20210
202-219-8743

Environmental Protection Agency
401 M St. SW
Washington, DC 20460
202-260-2080

Equal Employment Opportunity
Commission
1801 L St. NW #10006
Washington, DC 20507
202-634-9000

Export - Import Bank of the United
States
811 Vermont Ave. NW
Washington, DC 20571
202-565-3900

Farm Credit Administration
1501 Farm Credit Dr.
McLean, VA 22102
703-883-4056

Federal Aviation Administration
800 Independence Ave. SW
Washington, DC 20591
202-366-4000

Federal Deposit Insurance Corp.
550 17th St. NW
Washington, DC 20429
202-898-6996

Federal Labor Relations Authority
607 14th St. NW
Washington, DC 20424
202-482-6660

Federal Trade Commission
6th St. and Pennsylvania Ave. NW
Washington, DC 20580
202-326-2222

Food and Drug Administration
5600 Fishers Lane
Rockville, MD 20857
301-433-3285

Government Printing Office
732 N. Capitol St. NW
Washington, DC 20401
202-512-1991

Internal Revenue Service
1111 Constitution Ave. NW 20224
Washington, DC 20224
800-929-1040

International Trade Administration
14th St. and Constitution Ave. NW
Washington, DC 20230
202-482-2000

Interstate Commerce Commission
12th and Constitution Ave. NW
Washington, DC 20423
202-927-5350

Occupational Safety and Health
Administration (OSHA)
200 Constitution Ave. NW
Washington, DC 20210
202-219-8151

Occupational Safety and Health
Review Commission
1120 20th St. NW
Washington, DC 20036
202-606-5398

Office of Management and Budget
Old Executive Office Bldg.
Washington, DC 20503
202-395-3080

OSHA
*See Occupational Safety and Health
Administration*

Patent and Trademark Office
Washington, DC 20231
703-305-8341

Securities and Exchange Commission
450 5th St. NW
Washington, DC 20549
202-942-8090

Small Business Administration
409 3rd St. SW
Washington, DC 20416
202-205-7713

U.S. Treasury Department
15th St. and Pennsylvania Ave. NW
Washington, DC 20220
202-622-2000

U.S. Census Bureau
Federal Building 3
Suitland, MD 20233
301-457-2794

*Compiles comprehensive statistics on the
level of U.S. economic activity and the
characteristics of industrial and business
establishments at the national, state, and
local levels.*

U.S. Customs
1301 Constitution Ave. NW
Washington, DC 20229
202-927-1760

U.S. Department of Commerce
14th St. and Constitution Ave. SW
Washington, DC 20250
202-720-2791

*Acts as principal adviser to the president
on federal policy affecting industry and
commerce; promotes national economic
growth and development, competitive-
ness, international trade; provides
business and government with economic
statistics, research and analysis.*

U.S. Department of Labor
200 Constitution Ave. NW
Washington, DC 20210
202-219-7316

U.S. Information Agency
301 4th St. SW
Washington, DC 20547
202-619-4355

U.S. International Development
Cooperation Agency
2201 C St. NW 20523
Washington, DC 20523
202-647-4200

U.S. International Trade Commission
500 E St. SW
Washington, DC 20436
202-205-2000

U.S. Trade and Development Agency
State Annex 16
Washington, DC 20512
703-872-4357

Veteran Affairs Department
810 Vermont Ave. NW
Washington, DC 20420
202-273-5700

State Government

State Department of Commerce

Office of the Secretary of State

Regulatory Agencies

Department of Consumer Affairs

City and Local Government

Local Chamber of Commerce

Urban and Redevelopment Agencies

Other Sources

American Business Conference
17430 K St. NW, #1200
Washington, DC 20006
202-822-9300

Membership: CEOs of midsize, high-growth companies. Seeks a public policy role for growth companies.

American Chamber of Commerce
Executives
4232 King St.
Alexandria, VA 22302
703-998-0072

Managers of local, state, and international Chambers of Commerce. Provides members with educational programs and conferences on topics of interests, including economic development, management systems, and membership drives.

Legal Services Corp.
750 1st St. NW
Washington, DC 20002
202-336-8892

Minority Business Development
Agency
14th St. and Constitution Ave. NW
Washington, DC 20230
202-482-4547

Coordinates federal and private programs and resources to promote minority ownership of business.

National Business League
1511 K St. NW #432
Washington, DC 20005
202-737-4430

Promotes equal business opportunities for African Americans and other minorities; provides training and technical assistance, including loan procurement and marketing assistance.

Pension Benefit Guaranty Corp.
1200 K St. NW
Washington, DC 20005
202-326-4000

The Business Council
888 17th St. NW
Washington, DC 20006
202-298-7650

Membership: CEOs and former officers of major corporations. Serves as a forum for business and government to exchange views and explore public policy as it affects U.S. business interests.

National Association of Female
Executives
PO Box 469031
Escondido, CA 94046
1-800-634-6233

National Women's Business Council
409 3rd St., #5850
Washington, DC 20024
202-205-3850

Membership: The administrator of the Small Business Administration, Secretary of Commerce, Chairman of the Federal Reserve Board and six others as appointed by Congress. Reviews the status of women-owned businesses nationwide and makes policy recommendations to the president and Congress.

National Institute of Standards and
Technology
Route I-270 and Quince Orchard Rd.,
Bldg. 411 #A163
Gaithersburg, MD 20899
301-926-1559

Serves as the repository for information on voluntary standards for domestic and foreign products.

Library and Printed Materials

Reference Publications and Directories

Business Periodicals Index

A monthly listing of business articles appearing in a wide variety of business publications.

Directory of Directories

Describes of thousands of buyer's guides and directories.

Directory of On-line Databases

Provides information on databases and is indexed by product classification.

Dunn and Bradstreet Directories

Various directories that list information on various companies and industries.

Encyclopedia of Associations

Provides information on every major trade and professional association in the U.S.

Standard and Poor's Industry Surveys

Updated statistics and analysis of various industries.

Statistical Abstract of the U.S.

Updated annually, provides demographic, economic, and social information.

U.S. Industrial Outlook

Provides projections of industrial activity.

Books

Advertising and Marketing Checklists,
by Ron Kaatz

Business Plans to Manage Day-to-Day Operations, By Christopher R. Malburg

Creating Customer Value, By Earl
Nauman

Customer Satisfaction Measurement and Management, by Earl Nauman and Kathleen Geil

Do-it-Yourself Advertising, by Fred E. Hahn

The Handbook of Forecasting, by S. Makridakis and S.C. Wheelwright

How to Make Your Advertising Make Money, by John Caples

How to Make your Advertising Twice as Effective at Half the Cost, by Hershell Gordon Lews

Global Marketing Strategies, by Jeannet Hennessey

Guerrilla Marketing, by Jay Levinson

Lovers or Clients: Selling Succeeds, by J. Howard Shelov

Marketing Channels, by Louis W. Stern and Adel I. El-Ansary

Marketing Research: An Applied Approach, by Thomas C. Kinnear and James R. Taylor

Marketing Warfare, by Al Ries and Jack Trout

Ogilvy on Advertising, by David Olgilvy

Positioning, by Al Ries and Jack Trout

Services Marketing, by Christopher H. Lovelock

Total Consumer Service: The Ultimate Weapon, by William H. Davidow and Bro Uttal

Magazines/Newspapers/Journals

Advertising Age

Advertising and Sales Promotions

Adweek

Adweek's Marketing Week

American Demographics

Brandweek

Business Age

Business Horizons

Business Marketing

Business Startups

Business Week

Distribution

Entrepreneur

Fortune

Inc.

Journal of Advertising Research

Journal of Business

Journal of Consumer Research

Journal of Marketing Research

Journal of Retailing

Harvard Business Review

Industrial Marketing

Marketing News

Sales and Marketing Management

Selling

Standard and Poor's Industry Survey

Success

Venture, the Magazine for Entrepreneurs

Wall Street Journal

New York Times

Appendix C

References

Robert L. Anderson and John S. Dunkelberg, *Managing Small Businesses*. St. Paul: West Publishing Company, 1993.

Neil Balter, *The Closet Entrepreneur*. Hawthorne, N.J.: Career Press, 1994.

William H. Blades, *Selling: The Mother of All Enterprise*. Phoenix, Arizona: Marketing Methods Press, 1994.

Stephen C. Broydrick, *How May I Help You?* Burr Ridge, Illinois: Irwin Professional Publishing, 1994.

Bill Byrne, *Habits of Wealth*. Sioux Falls, S.D.: Performance One Publishing, 1992.

Peter Francese and Rebecca Piirto, *Capturing Customers*. Ithaca, New York: American Demographics Press, 1990.

Tony Husch and Linda Foust, *That's a Great Idea*. Berkeley, California: Ten Speed Press, 1987.

Jeffrey H. Gitomer, *The Sales Bible: The Ultimate Sales Resource*. New York: William Morrow and Co., Inc., 1994.

Alexander Hiam, *The Portable MBA in Marketing*. New York: John Wiley and Sons, 1992.

Thomas Hine, *The Total Package*. New York: Little, Brown and Company, 1995.

David H. Holt, *Entrepreneurship*. Englewood Cliffs, N.J.: Prentice-Hall, Inc., 1992.

JIAN, BizPlan*Builder*. Mountain View, CA: JIAN Tools for Sales, 1994.

Guy Kawasaki, *How to Drive Your Competition Crazy*. New York: Hyperion, 1995.

Philip Kotler, *Marketing Management: Analysis, Planning, Implementation, and Control*. Englewood Cliffs, N.J.: Prentice-Hall, Inc., 1991.

Charles W. Lamb et al., *Principles of Marketing*. Cincinnati: South-Western College Publishing, 1994.

Jay Conrad Levinson, *Guerrilla Marketing: Secrets for Making Big Profits From Your Small Business*. New York: Houghton Mifflin Company, 1993.

Herschell Gordon Lewis, *How to Make Your Advertising Twice as Effective at Half the Cost*. Chicago: Bonus Books, Inc., 1990.

Justin G. Longnecker et al., *Small Business Management: An Entrepreneurial Emphasis*. Cincinnati: South-Western College Publishing, 1994.

Christopher Malburg, *The All-In-One Business Planning Guide*. Holbrook, MA: Bob Adams Inc., 1994.

Allan J. Margrath, *Market Smarts: Proven Strategies to Outfox and Outflank Your Competition*. New York: John Wiley and Sons, 1988.

E. Jerome McCarthy and William D. Perreault, Jr., *Basic Marketing*, 8th edition. Homewood, IL: Richard D. Irwin, Inc., 1984.

Steve Miller, *How to Get the Most Out of Trade Shows*. Lincolnwood, IL: NTC Business Books, 1990.

Mary A. Molloy and Michael K. Malloy, *The Buck Starts Here*. Cincinnati: Thomson Executive Press, 1996.

Stephen L. Montgomery, *Profitable Pricing Strategies*. New York: McGraw-Hill Book Company, 1988.

James X. Mullen, "Be Quiet and Let Them Buy!" *Selling Magazine*, November 1995.

Patrick O'Hara, *The Total Marketing and Sales Plan*. New York: John Wiley and Sons, Inc., 1992.

David Parmerlee, *Identifying the Right Markets*. Lincolnwood, IL: NTC Business Books, 1993.

Murray Raphel and Neil Raphel, *Up the Loyalty Ladder*. New York: HarperBusiness, 1995.

Kenneth Roman and Jane Maas, *The New How to Advertise*. New York: St. Martin's Press, 1992.

Marilyn and Tom Ross, *Big Marketing Ideas for Small Service Businesses*. Homewood, IL: Dow Jones-Irwin, 1990.

John R. Rossiter and Larry Percy, *Advertising and Promotion Management*. New York: McGraw-Hill Publishing Company, 1987.

William F. Schoell, *Marketing: Contemporary Concepts and Practices*, 2nd edition. Needham Heights, MA: Allyn and Bacon, Inc., 1985.

Robert Shapiro, *Software Success*. Rockville, Maryland: United Communications Group, 1994.

William J. Stolze, *Start Up*, 3rd edition. Hawthorne, N.J.: Career Press, 1994.

Cort Sutton, *Advertising Your Way to Success*. Englewood Cliffs, N.J.: Prentice-Hall, Inc., 1981.

Leon A. Worthman, *Successful Small Business Management: Management Control, Accounting and Financial Management, Marketing and Sales*. New York: AMACOM, 1978.

Index